The 1978 Budget in Transition

The 1978 Budget in Transition

From Ford to Carter to Congress

Rudolph G. Penner
with Lawrence J. Korb

American Enterprise Institute for Public Policy Research
Washington, D.C.

Rudolph G. Penner is the director of the Center for Tax Policy Studies at the American Enterprise Institute.

Library of Congress Cataloging in Publication Data

Penner, Rudolph Gerhard, 1936-
    The 1978 budget in transition.

    (AEI studies ; 177)
    1. Budget—United States.   I. Korb, Lawrence J.,
1939-   II. Title.   III. Series: American
Enterprise Institute for Public Policy Research. AEI
studies ; 177.
HJ2051.P46   353.007'22   77-20996
ISBN 0-8447-3277-X

Printed in the United States of America

CONTENTS

LIST OF TABLES

PREFACE

This work was written at the American Enterprise Institute in the spring and summer of 1977. Its completion would not have been possible without the assistance of numerous government officials who provided technical information. I would also like to thank Colin Campbell, Robert Helms, William Fellner, Ronald Hoffman, Lawrence Hush, and Dale McOmber for their helpful comments without implicating them in the conclusions.

Special thanks are also due Nancy West and Joshua Rottenberg and other staff at the American Enterprise Institute for the preparation of the manuscript.

PART ONE
THE BUDGET AGGREGATES

1
INTRODUCTION

There is a widespread belief that public opinion is becoming more conservative. Liberals are supposed to be disenchanted with "big government," and those who advocate fiscal restraint are supposed to be in the driver's seat.

If there has, in fact, been a swing to the right, one would expect to find it reflected in the federal budget. Yet, President Ford, who made fiscal restraint a keystone of his domestic policy stance, was defeated, and almost immediately after taking office, President Carter added almost $20 billion to President Ford's recommended total outlay for fiscal 1978. In broad outline, the Democratic Congress enthusiastically supported the new president's additions to spending, even though the entire House of Representatives and one-third of the Senate must face the electorate soon after the end of the fiscal year.

Of course, election outcomes are determined by a multitude of issues, many of which are remote from the federal budget. Nevertheless, there is no other single document that provides a better reflection of our nation's priorities, and therefore, one might legitimately ask, What is going on here? How can higher spending be so popular in an allegedly conservative era?

There is no simple answer. Indeed, there are few questions related to the nation's budget that have simple answers. The numerous spending programs are complex; hard choices have to be made if spending is to be restrained. However, it is useful to put the matter into perspective by reflecting a bit on the alleged "swing to the right."

Public opinion polls and congressional debate clearly indicate that while "big government" may be becoming more and more of a villain, particular federal spending programs remain highly popular. During 1976, Potomac Associates found considerable support for increased spending on a wide array of domestic programs, such as "developing greater self-sufficiency in energy supplies," "helping the elderly," "combating crime," and "reducing water pollution."[1] The question leading to this result was carefully worded to indicate that increased spending would lead to increased taxes,[2] but this did not deter the respondents. However, the polling also indicated that although support for increased spending remains strong, it is eroding rapidly. Domestic programs had received much stronger support in an identical survey in 1972. The 1976 data also show a remarkable resurgence in the support for "total spending for defense and military purposes"—a shift that might comfort some conservatives, but one that will make total budget spending more difficult to control in the future.[3] Further evidence of a conservative electorate comes from an April 1976 Gallup Poll which shows 78 percent of the respondents in favor of a constitutional amendment to require a balanced federal budget and from a Harris Survey in the same month which found that "not raising federal taxes" is a major concern of 81 percent of respondents.[4]

These polls make it somewhat easier to understand the paradox in the apparent shift toward conservatism while particular programs retain considerable popularity. President Carter has, so far, found his way through this minefield by rejecting President Ford's cuts in particular programs while promising a balanced budget in fiscal 1981. The difficulties that arise from this strategy are explored in chapter 5, and it is far too early to predict whether it will be successful.

Although the differences between the Ford and Carter budgets (which will be discussed at length in subsequent chapters) allow some insights into differences between the philosophies of particular Republican and Democratic administrations, a word of warning is in order. The initial Carter amendments to the Ford budget and subsequent Carter program initiatives do not provide definitive evidence of the longer-run approach that Carter will take to the nation's problems. He simply has not had enough time to review the multitude of issues that must be faced in the preparation of any budget. There are approximately 1,040 domestic programs that must be considered along with hundreds of defense and foreign assistance issues. Ford's

---

[1] Edwin L. Dale, Jr., Donald R. Lesh, and Lloyd A. Free, *Priorities in an Uncertain Economy: Inflation, Recession and Government Spending* (Washington, D.C.: Potomac Associates, 1976), pp. 18–21.

[2] Ibid., p. 18.

[3] Ibid., p. 23.

[4] Ibid., p. 31.

budget was nine months in the making. Carter had only one month in office before he had to submit amendments. Even though he was aided by the most elaborate transition process in history, only a tiny proportion of the total universe of budget issues could be reviewed thoroughly. We shall have to await the fiscal 1979 budget for a clear indication of the budget philosophy of the new administration.

This monograph is divided into three parts. The first discusses broad issues, primarily involving outlay and receipts totals in the past and in the future. The second discusses specific budget issues in social security, defense, health, and in our grants-in-aid system. There are some significant omissions from this list. For example, there is no discussion of Carter's energy program which will have significant outlay and receipts implications in the future. At the time that this is written, the program is under consideration by Congress and it is far from clear what the outcome will be, although the matter will be settled, at least for the short run, before this work is published. There is also no discussion of welfare or tax reform. Here, it is difficult to predict even the broad outlines of the President's promised proposals.

However, these uncertainties do not constitute the main excuse for these important omissions. Practical considerations were much more persuasive. There is no way that one author can deal with all relevant budget issues in a short time period. The federal budget is simply too complicated for that.

The last part of the monograph deals with some recent and prospective reforms in the budget process. It considers the new congressional budget process and the potential for zero-base budgeting and sunset laws.

2
PAST BUDGET TRENDS

Has federal spending soared out of control? Is a growing tax burden dulling incentives and creating enormous inefficiencies in the private sector? A cursory examination of federal budget totals suggests that there is little cause for concern. The federal tax burden relative to GNP has grown little since the late 1950s. Total spending has grown somewhat more rapidly, but were it not for the recent recession this upward trend would be modest.

However, budget totals are misleading in that they mask certain more worrisome developments. The composition of total outlays and tax receipts has been changing more significantly than the aggregates and it may be the growth of particular programs and taxes rather than the aggregates that is disturbing taxpayers and causing a conservative reaction. Moreover, state and local government has been growing much more rapidly than the federal government. Perhaps most important, the federal budget is only one indicator of the role of the federal government in our society. Federal regulation involves little spending, but it has penetrated sectors of the economy that had little to do with government a decade ago. Federal credit programs which do not affect the budget totals have proliferated, and although the tax system raises little more revenue relative to GNP than it did two decades ago, it seems to grow ever more complicated. Each of these problems will be considered later, but first, it is useful to examine the budget aggregates.

Budget Aggregates

The growth in aggregate outlays and receipts is illustrated in table 1 for five-year periods since the late 1950s. Five-year periods

Table 1

FEDERAL OUTLAYS AND RECEIPTS RELATIVE TO GNP,
ANNUAL AVERAGES FOR SELECTED PERIODS
(in billions of dollars)

Fiscal Years	GNP	Outlays	Outlays as % of GNP	Receipts	Receipts as % of GNP
1956–60	$ 451.3	$ 82.8	18.4	$ 81.2	18.0
1961–65	581.0	110.6	19.0	106.0	18.2
1966–70	837.6	170.6	20.4	163.1	19.5
1971–75	1,235.8	257.2	20.8	235.0	19.0
1976	1,612.0	366.5	22.7	300.0	18.6

Source: *The Budget of the United States Government, Fiscal Year 1978*, table 21, p. 435.

are used in an effort to dampen the impact of the business cycle on government spending and receipts. This approach is not entirely successful because the last period, 1971–1975, was afflicted by both the aftermath of the recession of 1970 and the 1974–1975 recession which was the most severe economic decline since the Great Depression of the 1930s. Consequently, the ratio of spending to GNP is inflated slightly, both because spending on unemployment compensation and other income maintenance categories is inflated and because the denominator of the ratio, GNP, is depressed.

Total outlays climbed from 18.4 percent of GNP in the period 1956–1960 to 20.8 percent in 1971–1975. Although, as just noted, the latter ratio is slightly inflated, it would have exceeded 19 percent at full employment, while the 1956–1960 ratio of 18.4 percent would have been slightly lower. Therefore it is safe to conclude that there has been a very slight upward trend in the size of the federal budget relative to the size of the economy. In fiscal 1976, the ratio jumped to 22.7 percent. Again, this was almost entirely the result of the aftermath of the recession which both raised expenditures automatically on income maintenance programs and spawned a number of temporary emergency programs designed to deal with persistent high unemployment.

Receipts rose from 18.0 percent of GNP in the late 1950s to 19.5 percent in the late 1960s, but fell to 18.6 percent of GNP in 1976 as the result of major tax cuts inspired by the recessions of the early and middle 1970s. It is interesting to note that the 1976 ratio of 18.6 percent is equal to the average ratio prevailing since the Korean War. The slow upward trend in the spending ratio combined with the more or less steady receipts ratio implies, of course, a strong upward trend in the deficit relative to GNP.

Despite the slow upward trend in outlays relative to GNP, federal civilian employment has not grown relative to the population. Table 2 shows that the ratio of federal employment to total population in the 1971–1975 period was identical to that in 1956–1960. In 1976, both absolute employment and the ratio fell below the levels prevailing in 1971–1975. Since the labor force has grown relative to the population, federal civilian employment as a proportion of the civilian labor force was lower in 1976 than at any time in the period studied.

It is not easy to explain how a government that is spending a gradually increasing share of GNP is able to manage with a declining share of the labor force. Several factors have undoubtedly played a role in explaining this paradox, but their relative importance can only be a matter of speculation. There has undoubtedly been some increase in the productivity of government employees, although it is impossible to measure with any accuracy. It is generally believed that the rate of productivity increase in government is lower than in the rest of the economy, but it should be noted that a large part of the increase in total government spending has taken the form of transfer payments to individuals, and that the advent and improvement of the computer has drastically reduced the labor necessary to administer payment programs. It should also be noted that many of the expensive new programs undertaken in the middle 1960s, such as food stamps, Medicaid, and the expansion of welfare, are

Table 2

FEDERAL CIVILIAN EMPLOYMENT RELATIVE TO POPULATION, ANNUAL AVERAGES FOR SELECTED PERIODS
(in thousands)

Fiscal Years	Federal Employment[a]	Population[a]	Federal Employment per 1,000 Population
1956–60	2,369	184,854	13.5
1961–65	2,469	189,133	13.1
1966–70	2,833	200,706	14.4
1971–75	2,835	210,334	13.5
1976	2,832	215,074	13.2

[a] Average of employment and population at fiscal year-ends.
Source: *Special Analyses: Budget of the United States Government, Fiscal Year 1978*, table H-4, p. 168.

administered primarily by lower levels of government. In addition, the composition of the federal labor force has changed significantly in that the average skill level has increased dramatically.

It is also possible that government was overstaffed in earlier years and the civil service has simply been cut down to size. However, this hypothesis can be stood on its head: we cannot rule out the possibility that government is understaffed currently given the number of additional programs that have been created in recent years. Recent presidents have all resorted to more or less arbitrary ceilings and hiring limits to show their determination to get big government under control. Similarly the Congress tends to be much more stringent in authorizing new employment slots than it is in creating new spending programs. Consequently, we may be asking government to do more and more while giving it a smaller portion of the nation's total human resources. The result could be greater inefficiency and more dissatisfaction with government on the part of the taxpayer.

Composition of Budget Outlays

While total outlays would have grown modestly relative to GNP were it not for the recent recession, table 3 clearly indicates that the aggregate ratio results from opposing trends in defense and nondefense spending. In the last half of the 1950s, national defense outlays absorbed 9.6 percent of the national product, but by the early 1970s the relative burden had fallen by about a third to 6.4 percent and in 1976 to only 5.6 percent. In contrast, nondefense outlays have increased rapidly, rising from 8.7 percent in the late 1950s to 14.4 percent in the early 1970s and to 17.2 percent in 1976. Within nondefense outlays, payments for individuals—a category consisting of direct cash payments, such as social security, federal civilian retirement, and unemployment compensation; transfers-in-kind, such as housing payments and Medicaid; and indirect cash payments financed by grants-in-aid to lower levels of government, such as Aid for Dependent Children—have shown the most rapid growth, doubling in relative size from 4.1 percent of GNP to 8.2 percent in the early 1970s and rising further to 10.4 percent in 1976.

Those who are concerned about the growth of federal spending often focus on the payments to individuals category. Some do a simple extrapolation: using the 1950–1960 to 1971–1975 periods as a base, this one category will absorb about one-fifth of GNP by the

Table 3

COMPOSITION OF FEDERAL OUTLAYS RELATIVE TO GNP,
ANNUAL AVERAGES FOR SELECTED PERIODS
(in billions of dollars)

Fiscal Years	National Defense		Payments to Individuals		Interest		Other	
	amount	% of GNP	amount	% of GNP	amount	% of GNP	amount	% of GNP
1956–60	$43.3	9.6	$ 18.6	4.1	$ 5.8	1.3	$15.1	3.3
1961–65	50.0	8.6	28.4	4.9	7.6	1.3	24.6	4.2
1966–70	72.8	8.7	46.6	5.6	11.6	1.4	39.7	4.7
1971–75	78.9	6.4	101.9	8.2	18.5	1.5	58.0	4.7
1976	90.0	5.6	167.3	10.4	26.8	1.7	82.3	5.1

Source: *The Budget of the United States Government, Fiscal Year 1978, various tables.*

11

end of the century, or about as much as was spent by the whole federal government in the early 1970s. Others strongly assert that such extrapolations are extremely naive. They note that much of the growth in individual payments programs resulted from the creation of a number of new programs in the middle 1960s, such as Medicare, Medicaid, and food stamps. While these programs have grown faster than expected and faster than the GNP, it is often argued further that we are unlikely soon to experience another flurry of program creation like that of the middle 1960s and that the growth in participation rates is likely to halt. However, the alarmists are not mollified by this line of argument. They point to demands for welfare reform and national health insurance that are likely to be enormously expensive.

These contrasting views are explored further in following chapters, but first it is necessary to raise a more general problem. We must ask whether it is inherently bad for the share of GNP allocated to government to rise. The general folklore has it that the severe economic problems of New York City and the United Kingdom are the result of government spending gone wildly out of control, and some have attempted to document a negative relationship between the growth rates of various countries and the share of GNP absorbed by governments.[1] While such efforts are not without interest, the true relationship between the size of government activity and economic prosperity is extraordinarily complex, and it should be admitted that we know very little about it. However, a few obvious points can be made.

It is especially important to differentiate the question of the popularity of big government from its effect on economic growth. A government can command resources to further private economic growth by subsidizing private investment, technological change, and work effort, and, theoretically, it might even do all this in a highly efficient manner. However, if the populace is unwilling to sacrifice current consumption for greater future consumption, such a government may be highly unpopular.

Leaving the popularity of government aside for the moment, what can be said about the relationship between the sheer size of government and private economic growth? Obviously, very little. It all depends on what government tries to do and how well it succeeds.

---

[1] For a description of such efforts, see "Government Growth Crowds Out Investment," *Business Week* (October 18, 1976), pp. 138–39.

The analysis of the composition of outlays, (table 3) indicates that there has been a big change in what the federal government has tried to do over the past twenty years. In the period 1956–1961 over half of federal outlays and 9.6 percent of GNP were absorbed by national defense. By the period 1971–1975, national defense had dropped to less than a third of the budget and to 6.4 percent of GNP. This 3.2 percentage point fall was more than absorbed by a 4.1 percentage point rise in payments to individuals. The difficulty in generalizing about the relationship of government to economic growth can be illustrated by analyzing the possible impact of this one rather substantial shift in what government tries to do.

National defense may stimulate private economic growth some-what through its furtherance of technological change in ways that are valuable to the private sector, and often it contributes to public and private investment that can be used for nondefense production. But basically, its main effect under conditions of full employment is to deprive the private sector of resources that could otherwise be used for private investment and consumption. The cost may well be worth it, but obviously, the private economy is better off if international conditions are such that less defense effort is required. To the extent that higher defense spending lowers private investment, the economy's capacity for future private growth is also lowered. Similarly, the supply of labor available to the private sector is also lowered in a full employment economy by a larger defense effort. The increased taxes necessary to finance the defense effort may, in addition, have a negative indirect impact on work effort and on savings, but this effect is likely to be small relative to the impact of the loss of resources directly absorbed by production of the ships, planes, and so on, required by the defense establishment.

The impact of the growth in payments to individuals is likely to be very different. Because the system exists primarily to transfer resources from one group to another, the direct absorption of resources is very small, consisting only of the labor and capital necessary to administer it. In contrast, the indirect impact of the transfer system on the supply of resources through its effect on work effort and savings may be quite large. For example, it has been argued that the growth in the social security system has significantly diminished private savings without creating public savings to take their place, and that the growth in unemployment benefits has signifi-cantly dampened work effort.

In determining whether the current composition of outlays is more or less conducive to private economic growth than that existing twenty years ago, it is necessary to know whether the indirect negative impact of increased transfer payments on savings and work and labor resources to the defense effort. Given the current state effort is greater or less than the impact of the direct loss of capital of knowledge, it has to be said that no one knows for sure.[2] It is also necessary to ask whether government is inherently inefficient, regardless of its specific priorities. If it is, any expansion of government activity is automatically suspect, although not necessarily undesirable. This can be illustrated with a specific example.

It is clear that there are some good things that the private market would not accomplish efficiently if left on its own. For example, improvements in air quality are unlikely without some government intervention in private markets. Theoretically, an efficient government would assess the benefits and costs of different degrees of air quality improvement as best it could and use its tax, subsidy, and regulatory powers to achieve an appropriate reduction in air pollution. However, many argue that this is not how government operates. They envision a bureaucratic system in which individual administrators pursue power which is often measured by the size of their budget. As a result, there is always a tendency for government to go far beyond the point at which marginal benefits equal marginal costs and thus to overregulate and overspend. Consequently, whether government should engage in a particular activity becomes a question of whether the inefficiency resulting from the inherent tendency of government to go too far outweighs the inefficiency resulting from government's not intervening at all. As government expands into more and more areas, the opportunities for improving private market efficiency become more and more scarce even assuming perfect efficiency in the government. If the incentives created by a bureaucratic environment make it inherently incapable of operating efficiently, there is a strong case for limiting its growth long before all the problems of private markets are solved.

Where that limit should be is the fundamental political issue. When confronted by the obvious inefficiencies of bureaucracy, the liberal expansionist is likely to respond by advocating better "planning" and "management." The conservative restrictionist is likely

---

[2] For what it is worth, the previously cited studies suggest that an expansion in transfer payments is less detrimental to economic growth than an expansion of government purchases of goods and services (ibid., p. 139). However, the issues are so complex that any result of this type must be treated with extreme suspicion.

to believe that any planning or management system will be subverted by the bureaucracy into just one more instrument for enhancing its power.[3]

Composition of Budget Receipts

The most interesting development in the composition of unified budget receipts has been the steady decline in the importance of the corporation income tax relative to GNP combined with an inexorable increase in the burden imposed by the payroll tax (see table 4). The personal income tax rose in relative importance from 1956–1960 to 1966–1970, but major tax cuts in the early and middle 1970s reduced its importance to 8.2 percent of GNP, only slightly above the 8.0 percent prevailing in 1956–1960.

Personal Income Taxes. While the burden of the personal income tax relative to GNP declined between 1966–1970 and 1976, the aggregate ratios hide some important shifts in its structure and distribution. First, the tax burden in the late 1960s was raised significantly by the temporary Vietnam surtax. Second, GNP is not a very good measure of the relevant tax base. A better indication of developments in the permanent tax structure is obtained by taking the calendar 1966 ratio of personal tax receipts to personal income less transfers and comparing it with the same ratio in 1976. This ratio actually rose slightly, from 10.7 percent to 11.5 percent. The rise is a crude indication that the tax cuts of 1971, 1975, and 1976 did not quite offset the effect of inflation and real growth during the period which pushed most taxpayers into higher tax brackets. Moreover, some taxpayers were "indexed" very much better than others, and there have been significant changes in the distribution of the tax burden over the last ten years. The "typical" family has found itself in higher average and marginal tax brackets.

More specifically, the median census income for married couples with two children was approximately $17,000 in 1976, up from $8,000 for similar families in 1966. If it is assumed that the adjusted gross income for these typical families is equivalent to the census definition of income and if they have itemized deductions equal to

---

[3] For a bibliography and a much more detailed discussion of the relationship between government activity and economic efficiency, see my "Growth in Government Spending," mimeographed (Washington, D.C.: American Enterprise Institute, 1977).

Table 4

COMPOSITION OF FEDERAL RECEIPTS RELATIVE TO GNP,
ANNUAL AVERAGES FOR SELECTED PERIODS
(in billions of dollars)

Fiscal Years		Total	Personal Income Tax	Corporate Income Tax	Social Insurance Tax	Other
1956–60	Dollars	$ 81.2	$ 36.0	$20.2	$11.4	$13.6
	% of total	100.0	44.3	24.9	14.0	16.7
	% of GNP	18.0	8.0	4.5	2.5	3.0
1961–65	Dollars	106.0	46.4	22.4	19.5	17.7
	% of total	100.0	43.8	21.1	18.4	16.7
	% of GNP	18.2	8.0	3.9	3.4	3.0
1966–70	Dollars	163.1	72.6	32.5	35.7	22.3
	% of total	100.0	44.5	19.0	21.9	13.7
	% of GNP	19.5	8.7	3.9	4.3	2.7
1971–75	Dollars	235.0	105.1	34.9	66.0	29.0
	% of total	100.0	44.7	14.8	28.1	12.3
	% of GNP	19.0	8.5	2.8	5.3	2.3
1976	Dollars	300.0	131.6	41.4	92.7	34.3
	% of total	100.0	43.9	13.8	20.9	11.4
	% of GNP	18.6	8.2	2.6	5.8	2.1

Source: *The Budget of the United States Government*, various years.

16 percent of income, the average tax rate increased from 8.5 percent in 1966 to 11.3 percent in 1976. If the same assumptions are made for similar families with adjusted gross income equal to half the median ($4,000 in 1966 and $8,500 in 1976), the tax rate rose from 3.4 to 4.4 percent, while at 50 percent above the median ($12,000 in 1966 and $25,500 in 1976) the average tax increase was from 11.0 to 14.7 percent. In other words, the average rate for those in the middle income ranges has increased by about one-third over the last ten years, with those at the top of this range experiencing a slightly higher proportionate increase than those at the bottom.

The lower income groups have done considerably better. The income level at which families of four begin to pay personal income taxes has increased from $3,000 in 1966 to $6,860 in 1976 or from about 37.5 percent of the median income to 40 percent (assuming all income is earned income in 1976). More important, families below $6,860 in 1976 now enjoy a negative tax because of the earned income credit passed in 1975.

There has been a great variety of other tax changes over the last ten years that impacted different income groups differently. It is not within the scope of this brief analysis to document all their impacts, but a few generalizations are possible. If the goal over the last ten years had been to counteract the effect of growing money incomes, pushing taxpayers into higher tax brackets, it would have been necessary to increase basic exemptions, the maximum and minimum standard deductions, and all tax brackets by an amount equivalent to the increase in money incomes. Money incomes have somewhat more than doubled over the ten-year period, but except for a small adjustment for single taxpayers, tax brackets have remained constant. The basic exemption has increased only 25 percent, but has been supplemented by a tax credit equal to $35 per exemption or 2 percent of taxable income, whichever is greater. However, except for certain single taxpayers, the new tax credit combined with the increase in the basic exemption is not sufficient to offset the effect of the growth in money incomes. The minimum and maximum standard deductions have far more than doubled for most taxpayers, and in between the minimum and maximum deduction the percentage standard deduction has increased from 10 to 16 percent. As a result of these various changes, it is possible to generalize that singles and those who rely on standard deductions have fared best while very large families who itemize have done worst.

Of course, there is no particular reason for adusting the tax system to offset completely the growth in money income. Money income grows because of both inflation and real economic growth. It may be argued that increases in the total tax burden owing to real growth reflects a higher relative demand for public goods and services as people become richer. Increases in the tax burden owing purely to inflation are more questionable. In the 1966 to 1976 period, the tax system was more than adusted for inflation for low- and lower-middle-income families, but the upper-middle-class families suffered as they were pushed into higher and higher tax brackets. Only the standard deduction has been increased at a rate much exceeding the inflation rate.

It is interesting to note that 1977 tax changes again focused on improving the standard deduction. For married couples the maximum was raised from $2,800 to $3,200 and the minimum was made equivalent to the maximum for all taxpayers. It might be argued that it would have been preferable to give a break to those who itemize since those using the standard deduction have been treated so generously in the recent past. On the other hand, the 1977 tax changes have the advantage of simplifying the tax form significantly for those who can stop itemizing under the proposal and for those who would otherwise use the 16 percent standard deduction.

Other important tax changes in the last ten years have included the Tax Reform Acts of 1969 and 1976 which closed or reduced some tax loopholes, affecting primarily very high-income taxpayers, and imposed a minimum tax on certain types of income treated preferentially by our tax system. While these "reforms" have improved the equity of the system, they raise very little revenue and are not very relevant to the vast majority of taxpayers. They have, however, enormously complicated our tax laws. Other important changes in tax law since 1966 include the implementation of the accelerated depreciation range in 1971 and the increase in the investment tax credit from 7 to 10 percent in 1975. These changes have their largest impact on corporate tax receipts, but they have also benefited individual taxpayers with business income.

Social Insurance Taxes and Contributions. The fastest growing source of federal receipts shown in table 4 is social insurance taxes and contributions. The bulk of these receipts result from payroll taxes, primarily social security contributions and the unemployment insurance tax. Although the employer pays half the social security tax and the entire unemployment insurance tax, it is likely that most or

18

all of the payroll tax is eventually borne by the worker, either in lower wages or in higher prices for the things he or she buys.[4]

In 1976 the employee share of the social security tax was 5.85 percent of the first $15,300 of earnings. Since 1972 this wage base has been raised each year at the same percentage rate as the average wage increase of all workers covered by social security. All workers have borne the brunt of the increase in the employee's share of the social security tax rate from 2.0 percent in 1956 to 5.85 percent in 1976, but the middle of the middle class has suffered disproportionately since their tax base has increased more rapidly than their average incomes over the same time period. The rise has been particularly rapid over the last ten years.

If families of four earning $8,000 in 1966 and $17,000 in 1976 contained only one wage earner and he or she had wage earnings above the wage base ($6,600 in 1966 and $15,300 in 1976) in those two years, the average social security tax burden rose from 3.5 percent to 5.3 percent over the ten-year period. Added to the income tax burden computed previously, this means that incomes taxes plus the employee's share of the payroll tax rose from 12.0 percent in 1966 to 16.6 percent in 1976. The significant increase in the burden imposed by those two most visible taxes imposed on our typical family may help to explain the conservatism which is said to be afflicting a growing proportion of our populace.

The rapid rise in the tax base has, of course, made the payroll tax somewhat less regressive, as has the growing number of families with more than one earner. The distributional implications of social security taxes and the problems currently facing the entire social security system will be discussed in more detail in chapter 6.

Corporate Income Taxes. In the period 1956–1960 corporate income tax receipts were equivalent to 4.5 percent of GNP. By the 1971–1975 period this ratio had fallen to 2.8 percent with a further fall to 2.6 percent in 1976. In the earlier period the corporate income tax was the second most important in the federal system, providing almost one-quarter of total receipts. During the period 1966–1970 corporate tax receipts fell to third place, surpassed by social insurance taxes and contributions. By 1976 corporate taxes contributed only 13.8 percent of total receipts compared with 43.9 percent from individual

---

[4] John Brittain, *The Payroll Tax for Social Security* (Washington, D.C.: Brookings Institution, 1972), pp. 60–81. The Brittain methodology has been criticized by Martin S. Feldstein in "The Incidence of the Social Security Tax: Comment," *American Economic Review*, vol. 62 (September 1972), pp. 739–42.

income taxes and 30.9 percent from social insurance taxes and contributions.

The gradual erosion of corporate tax receipts relative to total receipts and to GNP has a number of explanations. First, the ratio of corporate profits before tax to GNP declined from 11.6 percent in calendar 1956 to 8.7 percent in 1976. This reflects in part a real decline in profitability and in part the more generous allowance for depreciation which resulted from the accelerated depreciation range instituted in 1971. The investment tax credit introduced in 1962 and liberalized in 1964 and 1975 has also eased the burden imposed by the corporate tax, as has the reduction in the highest marginal tax rate from 52 percent to 48 percent on earnings greater than $25,000 per year, which occurred in two steps in 1964 and 1965. Another corporate tax reduction occurred in 1975 as a result of reducing the corporate tax rate from 22 to 20 percent on the first $25,000 of earnings and from 48 to 22 percent on the second $25,000.

Although the corporate tax burden has declined in relative importance, the corporate tax still is not popular with tax experts. The corporation is a legal artifact. Tax burdens must be borne by people and cannot be borne by legal artifacts, but it is not clear which people suffer because of the corporate tax. Theoretically, it might be shifted forward to consumers or backwards to wage earners, or rest entirely on owners of capital. The usual presumption is that the bulk of the burden rests on owners of capital, but the case is far from proven.

Although the uncertainty regarding the distribution of the corporate tax is bothersome, it is not this uncertainty which is the cause of the unpopularity of the tax. The same sort of uncertainty also afflicts studies of the burden of other taxes, such as the payroll tax. Opposition to the corporate tax rests on the fact that it creates production inefficiencies in the economy as a whole. It does this because a higher tax is imposed on capital used in the corporate sector than on similar capital used in other sectors. As a result, capital is pushed out of the corporate sector, artificially lowering the before-tax rate of return in the noncorporate sector and raising it in the corporate sector. The entire capital stock of the economy could, therefore, be used more productively if some of it were shifted back into the corporate sector where the marginal rate of return is presumably higher on average.

The Ford administration proposed a partial integration of the corporate and personal income tax system to reduce the inefficiencies imposed by the corporate tax. The proposal consisted of two parts, each of which would be phased in gradually over a six-year period beginning January 1, 1978. The first would allow corporations a deduction against taxable income for dividend distributions; the other would give shareholders a tax credit against the individual income tax to reflect taxes paid by the corporation. At the same time, the individual's taxable income would be "grossed up" to reflect a portion of the profits earned by the corporation on the shareholder's behalf. When fully effective, the Ford proposal would have the effect of eliminating the corporate tax on earnings distributed by the corporation. However, it would not completely eliminate the corporate tax which would still be paid on earnings retained by the corporation. The proposal is extremely expensive: it would reduce receipts $14.2 billion in 1982.

Some might argue that the inefficiencies imposed by the corporate tax are not sufficiently severe to warrant such a large decrease in revenues given the political problems associated with any attempt to compensate by increasing other, more efficient taxes. Others would say that the Ford proposal does not go far enough because it does not eliminate the corporate tax imposed on retained earnings. They would advocate complete integration of the individual and corporate systems.[5] Carter has promised his views on tax reform in the fall of 1977. The way he chooses to deal with the corporate tax will clearly be one of the most interesting portions of his proposed reforms.

---

[5] A description of a completely integrated system can be found in U.S. Treasury, *Blueprints for Basic Tax Reform*, 1977, pp. 68–75.

3
FEDERAL ACTIVITIES OUTSIDE THE BUDGET

A number of federal agencies have been more or less arbitrarily placed outside the budget, even though their activities are conceptually identical to those of agencies still within it. Consequently, although their outlays affect the amount of debt that the federal government must issue and although they play an important role in reallocating the nations' economic resources, their activities do not affect the "official" estimates of the federal deficit or total "budget" outlays. It is difficult to explain this anomalous situation except with the cynical argument that these institutions provide politicians with the opportunity to bestow political favors without drawing the attention of the press and the public. However, before surrendering to this viewpoint it is important to note that the growth of off-budget activity has become a matter of some concern both to the executive branch and to Congress. The 1978 Ford budget recommended that all off-budget agencies be included in forthcoming budgets; the House Budget Committee made a similar, if slightly less sweeping, recommendation.[1] In its budget revisions, the Carter administration has said it will intensively review each of the off-budget federal activities and will make recommendations to Congress at an early date.[2]

The growing concern regarding off-budget activities is well founded. Their outlays have grown from a negligible level in 1973 to an estimated $10.8 billion in 1977. The list of off-budget agencies and their estimated 1978 level of activity as portrayed in the Ford budget is provided in table 5. It should be noted that the Ford proposal for an Energy Independence Authority, which was to provide debt

---

[1] House of Representatives, Committee on the Budget, *Off-Budget Activities of the Federal Government*, report no. 94–1740, 1976.

[2] *Fiscal Year 1978 Budget Revisions*, p. 16.

Table 5

ESTIMATED OUTLAYS OF OFF-BUDGET FEDERAL
ENTITIES, FISCAL 1978
(in billions of dollars)

Entity	Outlays
Federal Financing Bank	$ 5.9
Rural Telephone Bank	0.1
Housing for the elderly or handicapped fund	0.7
Pension Benefit Guarantee Corporation	—a
Exchange stabilization fund	−0.1
Postal Service fund	1.8
U.S. Railway Association	——
Energy Independence Authority	0.6
Total	$ 9.2

a Less than $0.05 billion.
Source: *The Budget of the United States Government, Fiscal Year 1978*, p. 30.

and equity capital on favorable terms for various types of energy production, was never adopted and has been withdrawn in the Carter budget revisions.

Except for the Postal Service, the Pension Benefit Guarantee Corporation, and the Exchange Stabilization Fund, the principal activity of the off-budget agencies is to make loans on more favorable terms than could be obtained on private markets. It is sometimes argued that because the government obtains an asset when it makes a loan, lending activity should be differentiated from ordinary expenditure activity and excluded from the budget. It is true that the economic effects of a loan are, in general, likely to be different from the effects of an ordinary expenditure of equal size, but this in itself does not merit excluding the total from the budget. Because government loans are almost always provided on more favorable terms than available privately and are often made for activities that would not be financed at all on private markets, the subsidy implicit in the loan does reallocate resources.

It must, however, be admitted that we know little about the amount of resource reallocation caused by individual lending programs. It is clear that different loans can have very different impacts: in some cases, where the same economic activity would have been carried out without a subsidized loan, the subsidy simply becomes a windfall to the borrower; in other cases, where the subsidy is essential to an expansion in the activity, the loan reallocates resources between sectors of the economy.

However, exactly the same point can often be made about ordinary spending programs. Some programs may simply substitute for private activity which would have occurred anyway while others may greatly increase certain types of activities, thus reducing the supply of resources to activities that do not get government support. In other words, the total amount of budget outlays, whether for lending or expenditures, may not provide a very good indicator of government's impact on the composition of GNP. That is not the role of the government's budget. Instead, it is an accounting document that shows total outlays, receipts, and the resulting impact on the federal debt. Consequently, if it excludes off-budget activities, its accounting role is not well-served.

Nevertheless loans, in general, are likely to have different economic impacts than ordinary expenditures. It might be argued, therefore, that net lending should be differentiated from ordinary expenditures whenever budget aggregates are published. This is easier said than done. Often the differentiation between loans and expenditures is ambiguous. For example, certain loan programs for agriculture and less developed countries contain provisions that make it unlikely that the loan will ever be repaid. Such loans might better be classified for accounting purposes as straight grants or subsidies.

For several years after the establishment of the unified budget in 1967, net lending was differentiated from expenditures in tables showing budget aggregates. However, difficulties of classification and a lack of public interest in the net lending totals led to the demise of this category. Despite the many conceptional and definitional difficulties involved in developing the category, the growing interest in credit programs may justify a reconsideration of the decision to abandon it.

Special Cases of Off-Budget Activity

Federal Financing Bank (FFB). Much of the growth in off-budget outlays is the result of the activities of the FFB, which was created in 1973 to improve the efficiency of federal government credit operations. Prior to its establishment, most of the government's credit institutions financed their lending activities by issuing their own debt to the marketplace. Although this debt had the full backing of the federal government, the agencies paid interest rates higher than those paid on ordinary debt securities of the government, probably because secondary markets for agency debt issues were not as well developed as those for ordinary debt issues, and perhaps because the characteristics of agency debt were less well-known. The FFB now issues ordinary debt securities and lends the proceeds to federal agencies to finance their direct lending operations. This has lowered interest costs to the agencies and has simplified the problem of federal debt management by reducing the number of different federally supported debt issues on the marketplace.

When the FFB makes a loan to an on-budget agency, which in turn uses the proceeds to make direct loans to the public, it would be double-counting to add the FFB loan to budget outlays. Therefore, the $5.9 billion in FFB activity shown in table 5 does not include such activity. Instead, it reflects FFB lending to off-budget agencies and FFB purchases of loans that are 100 percent guaranteed by the federal government. Guaranteed loans are loans that are financed privately, but the federal government promises to repay the lender in the event of default. When the FFB buys such loans it substitutes public financing for private financing, thus converting a guaranteed private loan into a direct loan from the government. FFB purchase of such loans is a matter of some controversy which is discussed below.

Government-Sponsored Enterprises. A number of enterprises have been established to carry out specialized credit functions that complement specific federal credit programs. Some, such as the Federal National Mortgage Association and the Banks for Cooperatives, were originally publicly owned but later converted to private ownership. Others, such as the Student Loan Marketing Association, were originally established with full private ownership. The term *government-sponsorship* means something slightly different in each case, but it usually implies government regulation of some of the organizations' activities and it can imply government-appointed officials on the boards of directors and/or the availability of favorable lines of credit from the United States Treasury.

Because of this close association with the federal government, investors attach low risk to the securities of government-sponsored organizations and typically lend at lower rates than if there were no government sponsorship. The ability to borrow at lower rates implies a higher level of activity than would otherwise occur and, in addition, these organizations often depart from pure profit-maximizing behavior to address perceived social goals. In other words, the existence of government-sponsored enterprises clearly alters the allocation of resources and it could be argued that their activities should be reflected in budget totals. Their outlays are substantial, estimated at $13.3 billion in 1978.

However, the president's 1967 Commission on Budget Concepts recommended that such agencies be excluded from budget totals, and the more recent recommendations of the Ford administration and the House Budget Committee followed suit. I believe this decision was correct because the enterprises are privately owned; it would be improper interference with shareholders' rights to subject their activities to budget review. It may, however, be worth considering whether the organizations' various linkages to the federal government should be severed altogether and replaced with an explicit subsidy system wherever it was deemed useful to induce them to serve public rather than purely private goals. In this way, the budget would explicitly reflect attempts to use these institutions to serve social ends, private ownership would be continued, and we would make explicit and implicit reallocation of resources that does not show up anywhere in the budget.

Guaranteed and Insured Loans

There are a large number of federal programs that guarantee or insure loans for certain kinds of economic activities. Under these programs, lenders are promised that the federal government will provide partial or full repayment of the loan should the borrower default. Occasionally, premiums or fees are charged for such protection, but they are often less than the full amount necessary to cover expected losses and therefore, the government provides a subsidy to the borrower. In other programs, guarantees are provided without charge.

By the end of fiscal 1978, it is expected that loans receiving such guarantees, over three-quarters of which are directly or indirectly related to home mortgages, will exceed $200 billion. In other words, the full faith and credit of the federal government will be providing partial or full protection for securities equivalent in value to over one-quarter of the national debt.

Because loan guarantees reduce the private creditor's risk attached to certain securities, they reduce the interest rate that has to be paid by the borrower. This in turn is supposed to increase the type of economic activity so favored by the federal government. Although extensive, this sort of intervention into private credit markets has not been intensively studied. Consequently, we know little regarding the impact of guarantees. If they are not effective, they may do little more than provide windfall gains to favored borrowers.

27

It should be noted that while a few guarantee programs may have a substantial impact on favored activities, their impact is likely to be neutralized as guarantees spread to more and more types of production. For example, if guarantees are confined to housing, such construction will almost certainly be increased. However, a brand new guarantee program for, say, student loans is likely to draw credit away from all other sectors of the economy, including the previously guaranteed housing sector. As more new programs are added for shipbuilding, energy development, and so on, the effectiveness of the older programs is sure to be diluted whatever their original impact. In the extreme, one can envision a situation in which all lenders receive some guarantee, and other than creating a bias toward more risky activities, there is little total impact on resource allocation in the economy.

Unfortunately, there has been little incentive to study the impact of these programs because of their low visibility. They do not show up in the budget totals except where premiums and fees provide receipts or where payments are made for defaults. These receipts and outlays are small relative to the total amount of loans outstanding. Also, authorizations to provide guarantees are frequently so liberal that they impose no constraint on the totals. The total volume is then determined in large part by the demands of the eligible borrowers.

Clearly, we shall not have a well-managed government until we gain more control over and insight into the impacts of these credit programs. At a minimum, a target for the total volume of guarantees should be included in the congressional budget resolutions. This would in turn require meaningful constraints on the authorizations for guarantees in individual programs. Guarantee fees should be charged to cover the expected value of losses, and where the Congress wishes to subsidize these fees, this should be done explicitly.

Guarantee programs should also be examined to see if 100 percent guarantees are ever necessary. Such a guarantee removes almost all incentives from the lender to check the credit worthiness of the borrower. Partial guarantees greatly improve the quality of the loan processing even if only a small portion of the total risk remains with the lender.

When the Federal Financing Bank purchases 100 percent guaranteed loans, financing it by issues of regular government debt and thereby converting the guaranteed loan into a direct loan from the federal government, it appears that any respectable accounting procedure would most certainly record the purchase in the federal budget. However, the issue is not quite that simple. If the purchases are put on the budget and therefore subjected to much more intensive scrutiny and control, there will be a strong tendency for agencies to try to avoid such sales as long as they are able to utilize relatively uncontrolled guarantee programs as a substitute. This will clearly complicate the Treasury's efforts at efficient debt management and also cause government guarantee programs to be financed less efficiently since the markets for some of these securities are far from perfect.

Thus, the issue of putting such FFB purchases on the budget cannot be considered apart from the issue of gaining better control over guarantee programs. This does not necessarily mean that the FFB purchases should not be put on budget immediately. Indeed the Ford administration decided on this step before resolving the issue of controlling guarantees. However, if implemented, it may mean that the decision will only result in a further expansion of guarantees unless steps are taken quickly to gain control of this largely hidden form of government resource reallocation.

Tax Expenditures

Our tax laws are riddled with special provisions that seek to encourage some forms of economic activity at the expense of others or that redistribute income to specifically defined recipients. Although the receipts losses associated with these special provisions have always been implicitly reflected in the budget receipts estimates they have only recently been listed in detail in the budget as a result of the Congressional Budget and Impoundment Control Act of 1974. While the explicit budget consideration of special tax provisions, called tax expenditures, is an important step forward, it is often argued that they are still not subject to the careful annual budget review accorded spending programs. There is considerable truth to this argument, but like most generalizations, it is often violated. For example, the investment tax credit, a major tax expenditure, has been reexamined and altered frequently since first introduced in 1962, while many expenditure programs are almost automatically renewed.

Tax expenditures can be loosely defined as special provisions of the tax code which depart from the normal tax structure,[3] but it is often no easy matter to decide which provisions of the tax code are "special" and which are part of the "normal" structure. *Special Analysis F* of the budget lists over seventy different categories of tax expenditure. While it is possible to have intense debates about

---

[3] For a more precise definition, see *Special Analyses, Budget of the United States Government, Fiscal Year 1978*, p. 119.

what should or should not be included in a list of tax expenditures, a large portion of the list is virtually noncontroversial, as is the fact that the budget should somehow record explicit government efforts to reallocate resources through the tax system.

There are a few individuals who argue that no taxes should be considered "normal" in that citizens should have a right to all of their income unless the law explicitly takes it away. However, it would be impossible to develop a "tax expenditure" concept consistent with this philosophy, and it would, therefore, be difficult to record the government's efforts to reallocate resources using the tax system.

In analyzing tax expenditures, one common error should be avoided: adding up the entire list of tax expenditures. One might then conclude that this is the amount lost by government as a result of special tax provisions. This conclusion is wrong. The amount associated with each special tax provision recorded in the budget assumes that only that provision is eliminated. When more than one tax expenditure is eliminated, the total gain can be more or less than the sum of the gains associated with each individual item. For example, if both the interest and the property tax deductions for homeowners were eliminated, the net gain in receipts would be much less than the the sum of the gains from eliminating each deduction individually because the elimination of both would induce many taxpayers to use the standard deduction. On the other hand, the elimination of the favorable treatment of capital gains would raise more receipts if the exemption of interest or state and local bonds was also eliminated than it would if it were the only tax change, because the two tax changes together would put some taxpayers into higher tax brackets than would a change in only one. *Special Analysis F* provides clear evidence of the importance of such phenomena. It notes that if all itemized deductions were eliminated, the 1978 revenue gain would be $21.2 billion, while the sum of all itemized deductions eliminated individually is $31.3 billion.

These estimates of revenue gain assume that the level and mix of GNP remain the same after the removal of tax expenditures. Since the intent of most tax expenditures is to alter the mix of GNP, the estimates are highly artificial and provide only a crude indication of the quantitative importance of different tax expenditures.

Regulation and Trade and Commodity Agreements

Regulation. It is doubtful that there is any area more responsible for antagonism toward "big" government than regulation. As a result of the creation of a number of new regulatory agencies in the 1970s, the degree of government intervention in the private sector has grown astronomically. The most important of these new agencies are the Environmental Protection Agency, the Occupational Safety and Health Administration, the Consumer Product Safety Commission, and the Equal Employment Opportunity Commission. All have noble goals which are shared by the majority of the populace. The problem has been, first, that the goals have often been pursued with little regard to cost or without a thorough exploration of the numerous different ways in which they might be attained. Second, the sheer volume of new regulations hitting businessmen at one time has made it extremely difficult and costly to achieve comprehension and compliance.[4]

Obviously, the fact that regulation is a device for reallocating resources outside the government's budget makes it no less costly to the economy. For example, a regulation that forces a business to install a piece of equipment to reduce pollution or to enhance worker safety imposes the same cost on the economy as if the government had purchased the equipment and raised taxes to pay for it. Only the distribution of the cost is likely to be different, but even this difference should not be exaggerated. In the very short run, much of cost imposed by a regulation is likely to be borne by the owners of capital, but once investment patterns adjust to the new rules, a large portion of the costs tend to be spread to workers and consumers. The final distribution of costs may not differ greatly from what it would have been if the investment had been financed by a broad-based tax.

I do not intend to imply that the resources conscripted by the great increase in regulation should have been captured instead through the traditional budget tools of taxation and spending. In some cases, such as in the pursuit of equal employment opportunities, this would hardly be practical. However, the fact that this effort has occurred outside the budget means that we are very vague about its total cost. We are even more vague about the total benefits, but this would have been true even if the budget had been used to attain the same ends.

While data on total costs are difficult to obtain, there is no doubt that the total costs imposed by economic and social regulation far exceed the costs of all of the other nonbudget activities discussed thus far. It has been estimated that the regulations of only the Environmental Protection Agency will have an additional gross cost of $40

---

[4] For a detailed discussion of these issues, see William Lilley III and James C. Miller III, "The New 'Social Regulation,'" *Public Interest* (Spring 1977), pp. 49–61.

billion per year by 1984,[5] although it should be noted that reduced pollution may also reduce some health and production costs. Meeting the noise requirements recently proposed by the Occupational Safety and Health Administration might impose capital costs of $18 billion.[6] The list could be expanded greatly, but it is clear that if all the costs had somehow been reflected in the federal budget, the apparent growth of government would have far exceeded that implied by the above analysis of outlay figures.

Trade and Commodity Agreements. Government can also reallocate resources outside the budget by using trade and commodity agreements. If, for example, voluntary import constraints are negotiated for steel and meat with other countries, the standard of living of American consumers is reduced just as surely as if a tariff were imposed. Similarly, commodity agreements that seek to stabilize and usually increase the prices of goods imported from less developed countries are a form of foreign aid in that resources are transferred abroad that might otherwise have been used to increase domestic living standards. If we are a major exporter rather than an importer of a commodity, such as wheat, an international commodity agreement which raises prices can, of course, be used to our benefit.

In recent years, it is hard to discern any important trend in commodity agreements. We have disposed of some agreements, such as those on coffee and sugar, and we have recently signed one in tin. The less developed world is now pushing hard for new commodity agreements, but it is too early to determine the outcome of the current negotiating effort. There has, however, been a recent wave of protectionism. Voluntary import restraint agreements have been pursued in items as diverse as shoes, television sets, and stainless steel.

---

[5] Ibid., p. 50.
[6] Ibid., p. 51.

4
STATE AND LOCAL GOVERNMENTS

While the federal budget has not grown radically relative to GNP, state and local government outlays and receipts have increased significantly. Although the federal government is not fully to blame for this growth, it has hardly been an innocent bystander. Total state and local receipts have grown rapidly from 9.3 percent of GNP in the period 1956–1960 to 15.2 per cent in 1971–1975 (see table 6). Receipts from the federal government in the form of grants-in-aid have grown more rapidly than total receipts, from 1.1 percent of GNP in 1956–1960 to 3.0 percent in 1971–1975. Put another way, grants contributed almost 20 percent of total receipts in 1971–1975 compared with 12 percent in 1956–1960. However, the state and local governments' own tax effort has grown rapidly over the same period, rising from 8.2 to 12.2 percent of GNP.

It is interesting to ask whether the rapid growth in federal grants has enhanced or dampened the growth in state and local tax effort. General revenue-sharing and other block grants, which are distributed according to a formula containing a tax effort variable, may have provided a direct incentive to increase taxes. However, the vast majority of federal grants share the costs of specific state and local functions. Because they make the function appear cheaper to state and local taxpayers, they have undoubtedly increased total spending on existing functions and, perhaps more important, have induced state and local governments to take on activities they would not have considered in the absence of a grant. However, it is not clear whether total spending on all the formal functions has gone up more or less than the total volume of grants, or in other words, whether they have induced greater or lesser tax effort at the lower levels of

Table 6

STATE AND LOCAL RECEIPTS RELATIVE TO GNP, ANNUAL AVERAGES FOR SELECTED PERIODS

(in billions of dollars)

Fiscal Years[a]	Total Receipts		Receipts from Own Sources		Receipts from Fed. Govt.	
	Amount	% of GNP	Amount	% of GNP	Amount	% of GNP
1956–60	$ 42.0	9.3	$ 36.9	8.2	$ 5.1	1.1
1961–65	63.5	10.9	54.6	9.4	8.9	1.5
1966–70	104.2	12.4	86.8	10.4	17.4	2.1
1971–75	187.5	15.2	150.4	12.2	37.1	3.0

[a] Fiscal years differ among governments. Budgets for each year before 1963 are by fiscal years ending anytime in the calendar year. After 1963, budgets are by fiscal years ending prior to June 30.

Source: *Economic Report of the President, 1977,* table B-74, p. 273.

government. Both results can be found in the econometric literature.[1] The issue is diffcult to resolve with econometric techniques because the structure and composition of the grant system has changed significantly over time, presenting state and local governments with a system of incentives that is constantly evolving.

Nevertheless, it seems very unlikely in the light of available evidence that the entire growth in state and local tax effort can be blamed on the federal government's grant system; it may in fact have been even greater in the absence of rapidly growing grants-in-aid, even though spending growth would have been lower.

Well over a third of the increase in state and local expenditures has been for education (see table 7). The baby boom of the 1940s and 1950s imposed significant demands that had to be satisfied to a large degree from state and local governments' own tax revenues. The sharp fall in the birth rate in the 1960s will provide significant relief which may be visible already in table 7. Although educational spending has continued to grow relative to GNP, it has absorbed a slightly smaller share of state and local budgets since the late 1960s. We can expect this trend to continue in the future, and even education's share of GNP may stabilize and decline, unless adult education spending increases.

Public welfare expenditures grew from 0.8 percent of GNP in 1956–1960 to 1.9 percent in 1971–1975, while highway expenditures declined from 1.9 to 1.6 percent of GNP. Other expenditures, which include health, sewers, natural resources, interest on debt, pensions, and other general expenditures, have imposed an increasing burden, growing from 3.6 to 5.8 percent.

Prediction of future trends in state and local finance is fraught with uncertainty. While education is likely to become less of a burden, expenditures related to the environment, especially sewage treatment, can be expected to grow rapidly. These expenditures will be lavishly supported by federal grants and need not impose a major burden on the state and local taxpayer. On the other hand, pension expenditures are also growing rapidly and do not receive direct support from the federal government.

While the financial difficulties of northeastern states and cities, especially New York City, have been well publicized and are likely to constrain spending growth, the relative prosperity of lower levels of government in other regions, especially those with energy resources,

---

[1] For a review of the literature, see Advisory Commission on Intergovernmental Relations, *Federal Grants: Their Effects on State-Local Expenditures, Employment Levels, Wage Rates,* 1977.

Table 7

COMPOSITION OF STATE AND LOCAL OUTLAYS RELATIVE TO GNP, ANNUAL AVERAGES FOR SELECTED PERIODS

(in billions of dollars)

Fiscal Years[a]	Total	Education	Highways	Public Welfare	Other
1956–60 Dollars	$ 44.6	$15.8	$ 8.5	$ 3.8	$16.4
% of total	100.0	35.4	19.1	8.5	36.8
% of GNP	9.9	3.5	1.9	0.8	3.6
1961–65 Dollars	65.0	24.3	11.0	5.5	24.2
% of total	100.0	37.4	16.9	8.5	37.2
% of GNP	11.2	3.5	1.9	0.9	4.2
1966–70 Dollars	105.3	42.5	14.6	10.3	37.9
% of total	100.0	40.4	13.9	9.8	36.0
% of GNP	12.6	5.1	1.7	1.2	4.5
1971–75 Dollars	185.6	71.5	19.6	23.2	71.2
% of total	100.0	38.5	10.6	12.5	38.4
% of GNP	15.0	5.8	1.6	1.9	5.8

a See footnote, table 6.
Source: *Economic Report of the President, 1977*, table B-74, p. 273.

is certain to result in some upward pressure on aggregate spending. As the overall economy recovers from the recent recession, the fact that states and localities are relying more and more heavily on progressive income and sales taxes implies that receipts will grow more rapidly than in the past; this, too, will facilitate more rapid growth in spending.

Major changes in federal policy could also have a dramatic impact on the well-being of state and local governments. For example, welfare reform and national health insurance could significantly alter the burden now imposed by Aid to Families with Dependent Children and Medicaid. Whatever the long-run prospects for state and local government, they will certainly play a crucial role in short-run attempts to stimulate the economy. A large part of President Carter's stimulus package—public works and public service employment, increased countercyclical revenue sharing, and manpower training— will be financed by increasing grants to state and local governments (see chapter 6).

The Carter increases go beyond the substantial growth in grants-in-aid already projected by the Ford budget. The Ford budget estimated a spending level of $70.4 billion in 1977 or a growth of 19.3 percent over the 1976 level of $59.0 billion.[2] Carter increased this to $72.4 billion, for a total growth of 22.7 percent. Ford would have drastically curtailed this growth in 1978 by recommending grants-in-aid of only $71.1 billion. Carter raises this total to $81.7 billion, thereby requesting 1977 to 1978 growth of 12.8 percent. This is below the 14.6 percent annual growth rate in grants-in-aid over the period 1955–1975, but it is still substantial. When added to the annual growth rate of over 17 percent between fiscal 1976 and fiscal 1977, one can legitimately ask whether such a two-year surge in grants-in-aid can be efficiently absorbed by the lower levels of government.

---

[2] This is not an annual growth rate because fiscal 1976 and 1977 were separated by a transition quarter as the end of the fiscal year was shifted from June 30 to September 30.

5

THE FEDERAL BUDGET, 1977 TO 1982

The 1977 and 1978 Budgets

The 1977 budget presented by President Ford in January 1976 had a loud and clear message on which he was to base much of his campaign for reelection: the federal government was to be cut down to size. His recommended spending level of $394.2 billion was about $20 billion lower than it would have been had the policies extant at the end of 1975 been carried forward. The American people were to be rewarded for this frugality with major tax cuts leading to receipts of $351.3 billion, also about $20 billion lower than implied by existing tax policy.

The major spending cuts were in domestic programs, although even defense spending was lowered slightly below levels implied by existing policy. Major domestic savings resulted from the substitution of block grants for categorical programs in child nutrition, health, education, and social services (see chapter 10). The Congress quickly rejected this program. Ford's major tax cuts were rejected and spending targets were raised about $20 billion in the First Congressional Budget Resolution (see table 8).

By January 1977 Ford was a lame duck president. Despite the rebuff of both the Democratic Congress and the electorate, the 1978 budget he submitted then repeated the major components of the 1977 strategy. This time the recommended outlay level of $440 billion was only $5.4 billion below the level implied by existing policy, but the call for a major permanent tax cut of over $14 billion was repeated. The result would be estimated receipts of $393 billion and a deficit of $47 billion.

When President Carter took office, the requirements of the new

Table 8

FORD, CARTER, AND CONGRESSIONAL BUDGETS, 1977 AND 1978
(in billions of dollars)

	Outlays	Receipts	Deficit
The 1977 Budget			
Ford (Jan. 1976)	$394.2	$351.3	$43.0
1st Cong. Res. (May 1976)	413.3	362.5	
2nd Cong. Res. (Sept. 1976)	413.1	362.5	50.6
Carter (Feb. 1977)	417.4	349.4	68.0
3rd Cong. Res. (March 1977)	417.5	347.7	69.8
3rd Cong. Res. Amended (May 1977)	409.2	356.6	52.6
Carter Mid-Session Review			
(July 1977)	406.4	358.3	48.1
The 1978 Budget			
Ford (Jan. 1977)	440.0	393.0	47.0
Carter (Feb. 1977)	459.4	401.6	57.7
1st Cong. Res. (May 1977)	461.0	396.3	64.7
Carter Mid-Session Review			
(July 1977)	462.9	401.4	61.5

congressional budget process (see chapter 11) forced quick action in formulating his spending and tax recommendations. Most of Ford's major spending cuts were rejected and, while Ford would have allowed the expiration of a number of "emergency" programs undertaken in response to the recession, Carter recommended their renewal in a "stimulus package" which he had announced in January (see chapter 6 for a detailed discussion). He in fact added to them to counter the economic slowdown that had occurred in the last half of 1976. Carter also rejected Ford's major permanent tax cuts, substituting smaller permanent cuts and a temporary tax rebate.

The net result was an addition of $19.4 billion to Ford's 1978 outlay level and an addition of $8.6 billion in receipts (see table 8). The deficit rose $10.7 billion. (A minor part of these differences is due to differences in economic assumptions and other estimating changes rather than to policy changes.) The Carter package led to 1977 outlays that were $4.3 billion higher and to receipts $13.1 billion lower than had been provided in the Second Congressional Budget Resolution. A cooperative Democratic Congress quickly accommodated the policies of the new president by passing a Third 1977 Resolution in March. Upon further reflection Carter decided to withdraw his temporary tax rebate. A somewhat less cooperative Congress reluctantly passed yet another Budget Resolution for 1977 to reflect the shift in policy.

As a consequence of these various policy changes, the 1977 budget deficit estimates went up and down like a roller coaster. From Ford's original recommendation of $43.0 billion, the deficit grew to a high of $69.8 billion in the Third Resolution. But by July, the latest estimates and recommendations of the Carter administration had lowered it back to $48.1 billion. The economic assumptions of the Ford and Carter administrations which underlie all these estimates are shown in table 9.

Given that the Ford forecasts were made in December 1976, they are remarkably similar to those made in Carter's Mid-Session Review. Economic forecasts seldom remain this stable over a six-month period. The real GNP figures are almost identical, but the unexpectably sharp fall in the unemployment rate occurring in the first half of 1977 allowed the Carter administration to be slightly more optimistic about unemployment levels in the remainder of 1977 and in 1978. A more significant shift occurs in the inflation rate forecast. The effects of the severe winter of 1977–1978 pushed up the 1977 forecast; Carter's

Table 9

FORD AND CARTER ECONOMIC ASSUMPTIONS, CALENDAR 1977–1978
(in billions of dollars)

Assumption	1977	1978
Real GNP in (1972) dollars		
Ford (January)	$1,331	$1,398
Carter (February)	1,334	1,406
Carter (Mid-Session)	1,330	1,399
Unemployment Rate (%)		
Ford (January)	7.3	6.6
Carter (February)	7.1	6.3
Carter (Mid-Session)	7.0	6.3
Consumer Price Index (% change)[a]		
Ford (January)	5.3	5.2
Carter (February)	5.3	5.2
Carter (Mid-Session)	6.9	6.1

[a] December to December each year.

1978 forecast has also been raised by 0.9 percentage points. The changes in the unemployment and inflation assumptions have opposite impacts on spending, impacting primarily the income security function.

A functional comparison of the Ford and Carter 1978 budget

Table 10

FORD AND CARTER COMPOSITION OF OUTLAYS, 1978
(in billions of dollars)

Category	Ford January	Carter February	Carter Mid-Session	Carter Mid-Session Less Ford Budget
National defense	$112.3	$111.9	$113.0	+$ 0.7
International affairs	7.3	7.8	7.1	− 0.2
Gen. science, space, & tech.	4.7	4.7	4.8	+ 0.1
Natural resources, environment & energy	19.7	20.5	21.7	+ 2.0
Agriculture	2.3	2.3	4.1	+ 1.8
Commerce & transportation	19.3	20.1	19.8	+ 0.5
Community & reg. development	7.9	10.0	9.7	+ 1.8
Education, training, employment, and social services	19.4	26.5	26.9	+ 7.5
Health	43.2	44.5	44.6	+ 1.4
Income security	143.9	146.5	146.5	+ 2.6
Veterans' benefits and services	18.3	19.1	19.1	+ 0.8
Law enforcement & justice	3.8	3.9	3.9	+ 0.1
General government	3.9	3.9	4.1	+ 0.2
Rev. sharing & general fiscal assistance	8.1	9.7	9.6	+ 1.5
Interest	39.7	41.8	41.7	+ 2.0
Allowances	2.7	2.7	2.4	− 0.3
Undist. offsetting receipts	−16.5	−16.7	−15.9	+ 0.6
Total	$440.0	$459.4	$462.9	$+ 22.9

Sources: Ford estimates—*The Budget of the United States Government, Fiscal Year 1978*, p. 372. Carter estimates—Office of Management and Budget, *Mid-Session Review of 1978 Budget*, July 1, 1977, p. 17.

outlays is presented in table 10. The largest absolute change occurs in the category of education, training, employment, and social services which contains a large portion of the Carter economic stimulus package. The increase of $7.5 billion is accounted for largely by the increase in public service employment and training programs. Carter also recommended in February an increase of $0.5 billion in the education function, and Congress added on $0.4 billion for higher education. The largest proportionate increase in outlays occurs for agriculture. This results from lower than expected agricultural prices and Carter's initiatives in increasing milk support prices and beginning a grain storage program.

The national defense increase over the Ford budget, which appears in the Mid-Session Review, is somewhat misleading. Some of it represents a "catch-up" in already authorized expenditures, owing to a major unexpected shortfall in defense spending in fiscal 1977. Carter's defense policies, which are discussed in detail in chapter 8, will result in a slight reduction in defense spending in the longer run.

Carter's Budget Projections, 1979–1982

The Carter administration released its first long-run budget projections with its Mid-Session Review of the 1978 budget on July 1, 1977. The projections, presented in table 11, are estimated on the basis of a highly optimistic economic scenario, one in which the

Table 11

CARTER BUDGET PROJECTIONS FISCAL 1979–1982
(in billions of dollars)

	1979	1980	1981	1982
Outlays	$ 498.6	$532.7	$564.8	$601.1
% of GNP[a]	21.8	21.0	20.3	19.9
Receipts	466.8	536.6	606.9	676.5
% of GNP[a]	20.5	21.2	21.9	22.4
Budget margin	$− 31.8	$ 3.9	$ 42.1	$ 75.5

[a] Fiscal year GNP estimated by author based on administration's projections of calendar year GNP.
Source: Office of Management and Budget, *Mid-Session Review of 1978 Budget*, July 1, 1977, table 16, p. 58.

economy gradually moves toward full employment while inflation continually decelerates. Such projections are not forecasts of future budgets. They reflect only the long-run implications of current policy as modified by the president's recommendations. Both because the economy is unlikely to cooperate and because there will be many important presidential and congressional policy initiations over the next five years, there is likely to be little similarity between the projections and actual budget outcomes. Nevertheless, the projections are vitally important: they reveal the base from which the Carter administration will have to work as it develops its longer-run budget strategy.

Like all projections of this type, the Carter projections show a rapid elimination of the budget deficit and estimate a huge budget margin of $75.5 billion in 1982. The single assumption most responsible for this result is that tax policy will remain constant. A constant tax law implies that the nation's tax burden will grow rapidly as inflation and real growth push taxpayers into higher and higher income tax brackets. This phenomenon is revealed in table 11 by the steady rise in the ratio of federal receipts to GNP, from 20.5 percent in 1979 to 22.4 percent in 1982, only a third of which reflects proposed energy and payroll tax increases.

In fact, Congress has tended ever since the Korean War to keep the ratio of receipts to GNP fairly constant by repeatedly "cutting taxes" to offset the effects of inflation and real growth. In fiscal 1976 the ratio of receipts to GNP was 18.6 percent, exactly the same as the annual average since 1954. During this period, the ratio reached a low of 16.7 percent in 1959 and a high of 20.8 percent with the Vietnam tax surcharge in 1969.

It may, therefore, be wise to alter the ground rules for making projections like those in table 11. If, instead of defining *constant policy* as keeping the *tax law* constant, we redefine it as keeping the *tax burden* constant, we get very different results. The current Carter tax policy recommendations (not including promised tax reform proposals) imply that the receipts to GNP ratio in fiscal 1978 will equal 19.6 percent, one percentage point above the long-run average. The implications of keeping the overall tax burden constant at the recommended 1978 level while retaining all other assumptions of the Carter projections are spelled out in table 12.

It may seem inconsistent to assume the same economic projection in the face of an assumed significant tax cut, as though tax changes would have no effect on economic growth. However, the long-run economic projections in the budget are more or less arbitrary and are not intended to be a prediction of economic activity given constant

Table 12

CARTER BUDGET PROJECTIONS WITH TAX BURDEN
CONSTANT, FISCAL 1979–1982
(in billions of dollars)

	1979	1980	1981	1982
Outdays	$ 498.6	$ 532.7	$ 564.8	$ 601.0
Receipts	447.3	496.1	544.1	591.7
Budget margin	$– 51.3	$– 36.6	$– 20.7	$– 9.3

Source: Calculated by author with data from *Mid-Session Review of 1978 Budget*, p. 55.

policy regardless whether constant policy is defined as meaning constant tax law or the maintenance of a constant tax burden. The long-run projections simply provide a base for making the budget estimates and for convenience, the same base is used in tables 11 and 12.

If *constant policy* is defined to imply a constant tax burden, there is no budget margin. Instead, a slowly declining deficit obtains throughout the period, even though the outlay projections assume no new policy initiatives in the period, 1979–1982.

Even in the unlikely event that there are no new programs or that new policy initiatives are financed by cutting back existing programs, the projections in tables 11 and 12 are likely to go astray because of economic developments not anticipated in the Carter assumptions. The key economic assumptions used to prepare the official projections are provided in table 13. The projections assume a strong, steady expansion from the recession of 1974–1975: the average real growth rate implied for the period 1975–1982 is slightly over 5 percent. Such an expansion is not impossible considering that we are emerging from the worst recession since the 1930s, but the odds are against it. We have not experienced a seven-year expansion that vigorous since World War II (although the 1961–1968 expansion came close). Even a minor recession between now and 1982 would put a major dent in the budget margins shown in table 11, under the assumptions that spending and tax laws remain constant, and a recession would probably inspire spending increases and tax cuts sufficient to eliminate the margin entirely.

On the other hand, if the economy does expand as vigorously in real terms as implied by table 13, it is very unlikely that Carter's inflation assumptions would be sustained. Although economists admittedly have little understanding of the relationships between inflation

Table 13

CARTER BUDGET PROJECTIONS ECONOMIC ASSUMPTIONS,
CALENDAR 1979–1982
(in billions of dollars)

Assumption	1979	1980	1981	1982
Real GNP in (1972) dollars				
Dollars	$1,468	$1,545	$1,621	$1,690
% change	5.0	5.2	4.9	4.3
Unemployment (annual rate)	5.7	5.2	4.8	4.5
Prices (% change)				
GNP deflator[a]	5.9	4.6	4.2	4.2
CPI[b]	5.7	4.5	4.3	4.2

[a] Fourth quarter to fourth quarter.
[b] December to December.
Source: Office of Management and Budget, *Mid-Session Review of the 1978 Budget*, July 1, 1977, table 15, p. 55.

and unemployment, few would bet that unemployment could fall as low as 4.5 percent without setting off a new inflationary spiral. Not much good can be said about inflation, but it does make it easier to balance the federal budget. Even though it causes spending to rise on indexed and other programs, receipts rise at an even faster rate under constant tax law as taxpayers are pushed into higher and higher tax brackets. Consequently, it is conceivable that inflation could push the budget margin higher than that shown in table 11 even if growth is lower than projected.

The Carter projections are also deficient in two other respects. While inflation is fully accounted for in the receipts estimates, only those outlays that are explicitly indexed are expanded with the inflation rate. Other programs are held constant in money terms,[1] which implies that they would constantly erode in real terms. Almost $15 billion in additional outlays would be required by 1982 to maintain all programs in real terms, if Carter's inflation assumption is accepted. Second, it must be remembered that there are numerous off-budget activities that are not reflected in the projection. If all the off-budget organizations described in chapter 3 were included in the projections, 1982 outlays would rise by $10–15 billion.

---

[1] An adjustment is made in the projections for federal pay increases which implicitly reflects the inflation assumptions made in the economic assumptions.

A Balanced Budget in 1981

Carter has made balancing the federal budget in 1981 one of his highest priorities, but he also realizes that this goal, viewed in isolation, is not very meaningful. Budgets can be balanced in numerous ways—some less pleasant than others. For example, an accelerating inflation rate would make the task easier, but no one, least of all Carter, wants to achieve the goal in this manner. Budgets can also be balanced by raising taxes either explicitly or implicitly as real growth and inflation raise the tax burden. This is not pleasant either, but Carter's budget projections and his explicit plan for eliminating the deficit suggest that some tax increase must occur if he is to achieve his goal.

Carter's explicit plan involves limiting 1981 outlays to 21 percent of GNP, compared with the 22.6 percent expected in 1978.[2] A balanced budget, of course, implies that receipts must also equal 21 percent of GNP, compared with the expected level of 19.6 percent in 1978. If the president's optimistic economic assumptions are accepted for the moment, the difference between 19.6 and 21.0 percent of GNP in 1981 amounts to a tax increase of almost $40 billion—over $170 per person in 1981 dollars. This is somewhat less than the increase in the tax burden resulting from a continuation of today's tax law, plus energy and payroll tax proposals, which implies receipts equal to 21.9 percent in 1981.

Putting the matter another way, Carter can propose a "tax cut" of about $25 billion from current tax policy and still achieve a receipts target of 21 percent of GNP if the economy behaves as projected. The key political question is whether he can restrict tax cuts through 1981 to only $25 billion. The basic problem is that Congress has typically acted to counter the effect of inflation and real growth on the total tax burden: that burden has not been as high as 21 percent of GNP at any time since the Korean War. A tax reform initiative will provide an excellent opportunity for Congress to lower the burden a significant portion of the way toward its historical average of 18–19 percent. The Carter strategy does allow for some new program initiatives. Current policy implies outlays equal to 20.3 percent of GNP in 1981, leaving room for almost $20 billion in new spending.

Of course, all this assumes that the Carter economic projections are realized. To the extent that heavy weight is given to balancing the budget, a perverse fiscal policy may result. The next chapter

---

[2] Richard J. Levine, "Luck and the Economic Game Plan," *Wall Street Journal* (June 17, 1977).

indicates that many are beginning to question the Keynesian theory that associates bigger deficits with economic expansion, but most experts still believe that at least a short-run relationship prevails. Consequently, a slowdown in the economy, which makes it harder to balance the budget, may induce the budget balancers to tighten up fiscal policy when a steady stance or a loosening is in fact called for. Conversely, an unexpected inflationary expansion may cause the budget balancers to relax when the need for fiscal stringency has in fact been strengthened.

6
UNEMPLOYMENT, INFLATION, AND THE BUDGET

Soon after taking office, President Ford recommended a tax increase to Congress. As the unexpectedly severe recession of 1974–1975 engulfed the nation, he soon withdrew his proposal and in its place recommended a tax cut. Even before taking office, President Carter recommended a tax rebate to counter a slowdown in the economy. About three months later he withdrew that proposal as the economy showed unexpected vigor in the face of a severe winter and the Congress became hostile toward the rebate. Thus the two new presidents quickly learned the perils of using the federal budget to "fine tune" the economy.

Approaches to Stabilization Policy

Over the past fifteen years, there has been a revolution in our attitudes toward fiscal stabilization policy. In the early 1960s, economists were euphoric. They thought that they had the world figured out and that it was Keynesian. It seemed a simple matter to keep the economy on a stable course toward full employment and price stability by judicious use of tax and spending policy.

Things began to deteriorate during the Vietnam War in the late 1960s. Economists found it was easier to persuade politicians to stimulate an economy than to slow it down. In the early 1970s they were further shaken to learn that there was no simple, stable relationship between the rate of inflation and the rate of unemployment. The most severe blow came with the failure of the economics profession to forecast the severity of the recession of 1974–1975. By then, economists faced the future with few vestiges of their extreme self-confidence of fifteen years before.

A final embarrassment was suffered during 1976 and 1977 by

49

those who would use the budget to control the economy. Not only do economists have a difficult time forecasting the economic trends, but the government has recently had difficulty forecasting and controlling its own rate of spending. In January 1976, halfway through fiscal 1976, outlays for the year were forecast at $373.5 billion. By March, the forecast as raised to $374.4 billion. In July, after the fiscal year was over, the estimate had to be lowered by $5.3 billion to $369.1 billion, but the final figures showed that even this estimate was in error. Actual spending turned out to be $366.5 billion—$7.9 billion below the forecast made in March with only three months to go in the fiscal year. The July 1976 estimate for outlays in the third calendar quarter of 1976 was $102.1 billion. The actual outcome was $94.8 billion—a shortfall of about 7 percent in one quarter.

These large estimating errors were due to many understandable factors, some of which involved the sale of assets and were of little relevance to economic activity. For example, HUD arranged an unscheduled sale of mortgages because interest rate conditions were favorable. More was received than anticipated from offshore oil leases. In other words, the bulk of the estimating errors were not due to bad management, but provided an honest reflection of the difficulties of controlling the timing and exact nature of the millions of individual decisions that eventually determine the spending total in any one year.

Although the difficulty of predicting spending has been a major embarrassment for the Office of Management and Budget, it is less important to the design of an appropriate fiscal policy than the problem of predicting the effect of changes in spending or taxation on economic activity. There have been a number of important challenges to the Keynesian theory which dominated the fiscal policy discussions of the 1960s. However, I think it fair to say that despite these challenges, Keynesian theory still dominates Washington policymaking. It provides the rationale for Carter's "stimulus proposals"; it underlies the policy analysis of institutions such as the Congressional Budget Office; it serves as a basis for the large econometric models that are used by policy analysts in the executive branch; and despite protests to the contrary, it shaped the way in which the Ford administration responded to the 1974–1975 recession.

In this context, I use the word Keynesian to describe those who believe that a sustained discretionary increase in government spending or a reduction in taxes will have a fairly predictable, expansionary impact on economic activity even if the monetary authorities hold the rate of growth of money constant. Almost all Keynesians believe that interest rates will rise as a result of the implied increase in the deficit, but the negative impact on housing, business investment, and consumption is considered to be minor relative to the demand directly and indirectly created by the government spending increase or tax cut. In other words, Keynesians tend not to worry much about "crowding out." The same rise in interest rates that may have a negative impact on nongovernmental expenditures is believed also to induce individuals and business to hold lower cash balances. The cash that is released finances increased economic activity and this serves to dampen the rise in interest rates caused by the increased deficit.

There are two major challenges to the Keynesian paradigm. The first comes from the monetarists, who can be characterized as those who believe that discretionary changes in the federal deficit have little effect on economic activity unless they are accompanied by changes in the rate of growth of the money supply. This result follows if the higher interest rates caused by the higher deficit have an important contractionary impact on private consumption and investment and/or if increased interest rates do not induce individuals and business to reduce their demands for cash. In other words, the increase in government spending or reduced taxes crowd out other forms of economic activity, and although the federal budget can be used to alter the composition of GNP, it has little effect on total economic activity or unemployment.

Needless to say, there is a wide spectrum of views within the Keynesian-monetarist continuum. Most modern Keynesians place great emphasis on the importance of the money supply while many monetarists believe that changes in the government deficit can have some short-run impact on economic activity. Furthermore, both monetarists and Keynesians may predict that increased deficits will have an expansionary impact because of linkages between increased deficits and the money supply. The monetary authorities may feel the need to support Treasury bond sales by supplying reserves to the banking system, and even if they do not, banks may increase the supply of lending and thus the money supply relative to cash reserves in response to higher interest rates. When the monetary authorities do not offset these tendencies, monetarists and Keynesians are united in predicting that an increased deficit will lead to an expansion of economic activity.[1]

A more recent development in macroeconomics stresses the role of expectations in determining economic activity. Monetary or budget

---

[1] For an expanded discussion of monetarism versus Keynesianism, see William Fellner, *Towards a Reconstruction of Macroeconomics* (Washington, D.C.: American Enterprise Institute, 1976), chapter 6.

officials will have a particularly difficult time influencing the economy in a predictable way if changes in policy are expected in advance or if once taken, they have a significant and immediate impact on the expectations of businessmen and consumers. For example, if decision makers in the private sector get the notion that a particular, expected expansionary policy will be inflationary, they may immediately move to protect themselves by raising prices and wages. As a result, the expansionary action may immediately create inflation without much influence on real economic activity or employment.

The government action need not even raise the expected rate of inflation to alter private decisions. It may simply cause existing expectations to be held with less certainty. This will have a direct negative impact on consumption and investment by making consumers and businessmen more hesitant to commit themselves to major spending programs, and an indirect impact by causing security prices to fall, thus making it harder for investors to raise capital. The 1977 *Annual Report of the Council of Economic Advisers* particularly emphasizes the role of the stock market in determining investment incentives. It notes that at the end of calendar 1976 the stock market valued the average company at less than the replacement cost of its physical plant and equipment.[2] Under these circumstances, the prospective return on a new physical investment has to be higher than in the past before firms will invest. In the absence of high returns, it becomes more profitable for the firm to use excess cash to retire its own stock. This phenomenon was dramatized in February 1977 when IBM offered to retire more than $1 billion worth of its own stock. With a higher stock market, it may have decided instead to purchase new machinery and equipment.

Because of such phenomena, it is obvious that expectations are crucially important to economic activity. However, the relationship between policy changes and expectations is somewhat less obvious. It was discussed by Keynes[3] but has not received much attention until recently.[4] This renewal of interest is long overdue and macroeconomic

[2] *Economic Report of the President, 1977,* (Washington), pp. 29–30.

[3] See the citation by Franco Modigliani, "The Monetarist Controversy or Should We Foresake Stabilization Policies," *American Economic Review,* vol. 67 (March 1977), pp. 5–6.

[4] The discussion above emphasizes the response of expectations to a given policy change. The recent literature places more emphasis on the fact that the policies themselves may be predicted and then immediately neutralized by individual actions. (See T. J. Sargent and N. Wallace, "Rational Expectations, the Optimal Monetary Instrument and the Optimal Money Supply Rule," *Journal of Political Economy,* vol. 83 (April 1975), pp. 241–57. A more complete bibliography can be found in Modigliani, "The Monetarist Controversy," pp. 18–19.)

policy makers can ignore the new literature only at their own peril: it may make them obsolete.

There is yet another challenge to traditional Keynesian theory that has recently been popularized by the *Wall Street Journal* on the basis of theoretical work by Robert Mundell and Arthur Laffer. It is argued that traditional Keynesians pay insufficient attention to the effect of taxation on the supply of goods and services. Mundell and Laffer believe that tax cuts have a major stimulative impact on production. While this possibility has long been recognized, it is not thought to be of major quantitative significance by most macroeconomists.

If, despite the challenges to the traditional Keynesian view of the world, one continues to accept the notion that the federal budget can be used to alter aggregate demand, important questions arise as to how the assumed power of the budget should be used. For example, what unemployment rate should we aim for and how fast can we approach it?

Since the early 1960s an unemployment rate of 4.0 percent has been more or less arbitrarily used as a definition of "full employment." The full-employment unemployment rate can be seen as the rate below which inflationary pressures begin to accelerate. Until this year, official concepts such as the full employment budget and potential GNP were all calculated assuming unemployment rate of 4 percent. In early 1977 Ford's Council of Economic Advisers took the important step of changing this definition. They noted that labor force composition has changed significantly over the last two decades as teenage and female workers have become more numerous. Since these groups typically experience high rates of unemployment relative to other members of the labor force, their growing numbers imply that a given degree of labor market "tightness" must now be associated with a higher unemployment rate than it was twenty years ago. Because of these demographic changes, the CEA estimated that an unemployment rate of 4.9 percent in 1977 was equivalent to 4.0 percent rate in 1955. They also noted that the growing generosity of unemployment compensation and other factors may have raised the full-employment unemployment rate further, "perhaps, closer to 5.5 percent," but no explicit adjustment was made for such factors. The potential GNP and the full-employment budget were estimated at levels consistent with a 4.9 percent unemployment rate.[5]

---

[5] *Economic Report of the President, 1977*, pp. 48–51. Phillip Cagan estimates that the noninflationary unemployment rate is now between 5.8 and 6.2 percent. See, "The Reduction of Inflation and the Magnitude of Unemployment," *Contemporary Economic Problems, 1977*, William Fellner, ed. (American Enterprise Institute, Washington, D.C.: 1977), pp. 15–52.

The Carter administration has implicitly rejected the Ford CEA's reestimate of potential GNP. The Carter long-run economic projections, discussed in chapter 5, assume an unemployment rate of 4.4 percent in the last quarter of 1982. The demographic adjustments made by the Ford CEA imply a full employment rate of 4.7 percent at that time. Needless to say, there is much uncertainty on such matters and the 0.3 percentage point difference between the Ford and Carter goals is not large relative to this range of uncertainty. Full employment does not represent a rigid ceiling that cannot be exceeded and the Carter administration clearly hopes that manpower policies can lower the full-employment unemployment rate. However, the Ford definition of full employment was itself highly optimistic; it is hard to avoid the concern that, if it were pursued, the Carter unemployment rate goal of 4.4 percent would be highly inflationary.

However, there is little to worry about yet. Even with the optimistic Carter economic projections, unemployment rates below 6.0 percent are not achieved until 1979. Carter's programs to lower unemployment to this level are discussed below, but first, it may be useful to clarify some confusions that arise whenever "stimulus" packages are discussed.

Confusion 1—the difference between creating a job and increasing employment. Whenever a program is proposed to reduce unemployment, the first question asked by politicians and the press is, "How many jobs will it create?" Any astute proponent of a program will have a precise answer readily available. Thus, Congressman Wright, in a discussing a $2 billion appropriation for public works, estimated that it would create 150,000 on-site jobs and possibly as many as 150,000 off-site jobs. But, in opposing public works spending, Ford stated with equal certainty that the effect on employment per dollar of spending would be less than one-quarter of this amount.[6] Such a large discrepancy exists between the two estimates because they probably refer to quite different concepts, and there is a variety of concepts from which to choose.

If one wishes to find a very high job impact, one can define the word "job" to refer to any task associated with a project. A specific task can take several hours, as in the case of an electrician hired to inspect the wiring in a new public building, or several years, as in the case of a laborer hired for the duration of the construction period.[7]

---

[6] *Presidential Documents, Gerald R. Ford, 1976* (July 6, 1976), p. 1139.

[7] For an excellent discussion of such distinctions, see Robert J. Samuelson, "The Never Ending Jobs Program Debate . . . How Many Jobs and at What Price," *National Journal*, vol. 9 (February 12, 1977), pp. 248–49.

A somewhat more useful concept involves the number of worker-years of employment generated by a specific appropriation.[8] However, even this concept has its deficiencies. For example, if two worker-years of employment are generated, it is obviously of some importance whether this means employment for two new workers for one year, one new worker for two years, or forty already-employed workers for two extra hours a week. Probably the most useful concept for stabilization purposes involves estimating the project's total impact on employment at specific times, say the end of 1977 and the end of 1978. Needless to say, making such estimates involves enormous uncertainty and anyone who makes them confidently should be viewed with extreme suspicion.

Confusion 2—the difference between increasing employment and reducing unemployment. It is important not to assume that those employed as a result of a government action are all drawn from the ranks of the unemployed. Any improvement in employment will draw new people into the labor force. The Congressional Budget Office estimates that of every ten people employed as a result of a tax cut, six will come from the ranks of the unemployed and four will be new entrants to the labor force.[9] The CBO believes that the induced labor force increases will be less where a program is focused on the unemployed population, but this is not clear since anything that depletes the ranks of the unemployed would be expected to reduce the time required to search for jobs and thereby to attract new labor force entrants. To the extent that unemployment is reduced, it is also important not to assume that there is a one-for-one reduction in unemployment benefit payments. Fewer than 60 percent of the unemployed are covered by benefit programs.

Confusion 3—the difference between raising federal spending and raising total spending. Often, the public discussion of new spending programs seems to imply that all government spending can be thought of as an add-on to total spending and that, consequently, all employment associated with a government project represents a net add-on to total employment. The extent to which this is true is at the core of the dispute between monetarists and Keynesians, with the former believing that any gain in employment resulting directly from a change in budget policy will be offset indirectly by reductions

---

[8] A number of different techniques exist for making such estimates. For example, see Diane S. Finger, "Labor Requirements for Federal Highway Construction," *Monthly Labor Review* (December 1975), pp. 31ff.

[9] Congressional Budget Office, *Temporary Measures to Stimulate Employment: An Evaluation of Some Alternatives*, p. 98.

in employment in the private sector as government spending crowds out other forms of economic activity.

However, even within the Keynesian model of the economy, there is room for uncertainty on this issue. To a Keynesian, it is vitally important how much of a federal expenditure or tax reduction is initially saved by the beneficiaries. This point will be discussed in some detail below with reference to the specific components of the Carter stimulus package. Here it is sufficient to note that there is considerable dispute regarding the impact of temporary tax cuts and grants-in-aid on total spending. If a temporary tax cut is all saved, nothing much happens. Increased private saving simply offsets increased government dissaving. Heuristically, one can think of the recipients simply using their new savings to buy the government debt issues necessary to finance the tax cut. In fact, the chain linking the new savings and the purchase of debt issues is likely to be much more complex and involve a number of financial intermediaries, but the result is the same. Similarly, if grants-in-aid are used by state and local governments to finance activities that they would have undertaken anyway, or in other words, if the federal largess is used to reduce state and local deficits, an increased federal deficit simply replaces state and local deficits and not much happens to economic activity. If the financial relief provided by grants-in-aid is used to lower state and local taxes, the result is similar to that of a federal tax cut.

The Carter Stimulus Package

The first budget revisions submitted by President Carter in February 1977 recommended increases of $10.8 billion in both the fiscal 1977 and fiscal 1978 deficits above the levels recommended by President Ford. A part of the overall Carter program was segregated out and labeled his "stimulus" package. It consisted of $15.7 billion in tax cuts and outlay increases in fiscal 1977 and $15.9 billion in 1978.

The amounts in the stimulus package are larger than the increases in the deficit for two major reasons. First, the stimulus package was assumed to lead to a more ebullient economy which would allow the government to recoup some of the increased spending and tax cuts. Second, Carter provided less of a permanent tax cut than was provided by Ford, whose 1978 budget also contained considerable "stimulus" for both 1977 and 1978. There were, of course, a number of other cuts and add-ons and some changes in spending estimates which also affected the recommended deficits.

Those deficits ended up at $68.0 billion in 1977 and $57.7 billion in 1978. The $68.0 billion deficit in 1977 was $1.5 billion larger than the 1976 deficit and represented a significant shift toward stimulus. With no policy changes, the deficit would have fallen to less than $40 billion. Once the rebate was withdrawn in April, however, the fiscal policy stance, as measured by the deficit, changed significantly. Other policy changes, congressional actions, and estimating changes also affected the deficit, and by July the administration was estimating a deficit of only $48.1 billion in 1977 and $61.5 billion in 1978. This left them in the awkward position of recommending a significant increase in the unified deficit between 1977 and 1978 while the economy was expanding vigorously.

Fiscal policy appears a little less destabilizing if the national income accounting (NIA) version of the budget is examined. This accounting concept is the one usually used by economists when measuring the impact of the budget in the economy. The NIA deficit, consistent with the administration's July estimates, rises only slightly from $51.8 billion in fiscal 1977 to $54.0 billion in fiscal 1978.

A summary of the components of the stimulus package, as it was originally proposed, appears in table 14. The spirit in which they were proposed was Keynesian, but Carter's vacillation over the nature of the stimulus package may provide expectations theorists with an excellent opportunity for testing their hypotheses. After the package was announced, the stock market started a long decline that destroyed far more wealth than could possibly be created by the policy. Treasury

Table 14

CARTER STIMULUS PROPOSALS, FEBRUARY 1977
(in billions of dollars)

Item	1977 Impact	1978 Impact
$50 rebates and payments	$11.4	—
Changes in the standard deduction	1.5	$ 5.7
Business tax incentives	.9	2.4
Public service employment	.7	3.4
Expanded training and youth programs	.3	1.6
Accelerated public works	.2	2.0
Increased countercyclical revenue sharing	.7	.7
Total receipts and outlays	$15.7	$15.9

Source: Office of Management and Budget, *Fiscal Year 1978 Budget Revisions*, February 1977, p. 12.

bill futures rates also rose significantly.[10] The day the rebate was withdrawn the stock market actually rose. No direct causal relationship between the policy changes and various measures of the state of investor expectations has been proved, but the coincidence of events is at least suggestive. It may be that any potential beneficial impact of the package was nullified by investor expectations that it posed an inflationary danger; that is, the negative indirect effect on business investment may have offset any direct increase in demand created by the program.

Fifty-Dollar Rebates and Payments. Even though the temporary rebate was eventually withdrawn, it merits analysis because such plans are sure to be considered in the future whenever the economy slows down. The original proposal involved a $50 per person rebate of 1976 taxes for all taxpayers and their dependents plus a $50 payment to recipients of social security, supplemental security income, railroad retirement, and the earned income credit. The program was valued at $11.4 billion.

Carter originally chose to seek economic stimulus largely through a temporary, one-shot payment rather than through a permanent tax cut so that future receipts would not be eroded, thus leaving more financial resources in the long run to lower the deficit and/or finance new programs. Rebates of prior-year taxes also have the advantage that they can be paid out quickly—all in one lump sum. A permanent or even a temporary cut in current-year taxes would usually be implemented by lowering withholding rates and would, therefore, be paid out gradually over the year.

There is, however, considerable dispute over the impact of a temporary tax change on consumer spending. Economists generally accept the permanent income theory of consumption which states that in a world of perfect capital markets, a person's consumption will depend on expectations of income over his or her lifetime. Since a one-shot tax rebate does not have a large impact on long-run expected income, it should not have much impact on short-run consumption. However, capital markets are not perfect and individuals may with some reason believe that one rebate may be the precursor of others in the future. Consequently, a rebate may have significantly more impact than is suggested by a pure permanent income theory.

---

[10] A. E. Burger, R. W. Long, and R. H. Roache, "The Treasury Bill Futures Market and Market Expectations of Interest Rates," *Federal Reserve Bank of St. Louis Review*, vol. 59 (June 1977), p. 9.

Studies of past temporary tax changes are not very illuminating. Temporary tax increases or decreases are usually undertaken when the economy is being buffeted by other major forces, for instance, during the Korean and Vietnam wars and near the trough of the 1974–1975 recession, and it is very difficult to disentangle the impact of the tax change from the impact of other variables that are changing simultaneously. Consequently, economists are still debating the impact of the temporary Vietnam income tax surcharge, with Okun arguing that it had a major impact on consumption[11] and Springer vigorously disputing that conclusion.[12] The temporary tax rebate of 1975 has not yet been studied extensively, but after considerable discussion of the problem of isolating its effects, Chase Econometrics concluded that somewhat less than half the rebate was spent,[13] about a third less than would be spent out of a permanent tax cut of similar magnitude. Roughly speaking, the Chase Econometric results are similar to those of the Congressional Budget Office whose estimates imply that a temporary rebate has about two-thirds as much impact on spending as a permanent tax cut.[14] The similarity of results is not surprising and does not really provide independent evidence, since the CBO uses a model of the world that is similar in approach to that of Chase Econometrics.

To the extent that spending is stimulated by a temporary rebate, everyone would agree that the impact is very short-lived. The rate of economic expansion will at first be more rapid than without the rebate. But once the rebate is spent, spending falls to more normal levels, and for a short period, the rate of expansion is actually slower than if the rebate had not occurred. This creates a danger that the subsequent slowdown in the economy will be misinterpreted as a signal that the recovery is fundamentally weak and hence requires even more stimulus. As a result, policies could become highly erratic unless considerable self-restraint is applied.

---

[11] A. M. Okun, "The Personal Tax Surcharge and Consumer Demand, 1968–70," *Brookings Papers on Economic Activity 1971*, no. 1 (Washington, D.C.), pp. 167–212.

[12] W. L. Springer, "Did the 1968 Surcharge Really Work?" *American Economic Review*, vol. 65 (September 1975), pp. 644–58. See also the comments by Okun and Springer in *American Economic Review*, vol. 67 (March 1977), pp. 166–72.

[13] Chase Econometrics, "Analysis," *Forecasts of March 25, 1977* (New York, 1977) pp. 2–6.

[14] Congressional Budget Office, *Short-Run Measures to Stimulate the Economy* (Washington, D.C., March 1977), p. 3.

Permanent Tax Reductions. Carter proposed a flat standard deduction of $2,200 for single persons and $3,000 for married couples to replace the current complex system of minimum, maximum, and percentage standard deductions. He also proposed to extend the $35 per exemption tax credit to the aged and blindness exemptions. The former proposal would greatly simplify the calculation of the standard deduction for those who already use it, and will allow some taxpayers to switch from itemizing to the simpler task of taking a standard deduction. The latter proposal would greatly simplify the preparation of tax returns by allowing a much greater use of tables. The revenue cost of the proposal is $1.5 billion in fiscal 1977 and $5.7 billion in fiscal 1978. Congress modified the proposal and increased the standard deduction single returns to $2,400 and for joint returns to $3,200 rather than the $3,000 proposed by Carter.

In addition to simplifying tax forms greatly, it has already been noted that permanent tax reductions are more likely than temporary rebates to increase consumer spending. In addition, by slightly reducing marginal tax rates for those who do not itemize, the Carter proposal may have a salutary impact on work effort and economic efficiency.

If one grants that some permanent tax cut was warranted, there are only two significant disadvantages to this proposal. The first involves equity. Over the last ten years, the standard deduction has been increased at a much more rapid rate than any other component of the personal income tax system, while the tax rate structure for joint returns has remained constant since 1965 and the tax rate structure for singles has been made only slightly more generous. As a result, those who benefit from the standard deduction have, generally, been treated generously relative to those who itemize. The itemizer may have a just claim on more relief from the higher marginal rates that have resulted as inflation and real growth have pushed them into higher marginal tax brackets more rapidly than it has those who use the standard deduction. Second, increases in the standard deduction reduce the power of those itemized deductions or tax expenditures that have been designed to encourage certain types of economic activity, such as charitable donations. There is, of course, considerable dispute about the merits of the many special deductions embodied in our tax law, and to many observers, anything that reduces their power is desirable.

Carter also proposed a permanent reduction in business taxes in the form of either a 2 percentage point increase in the current investment tax credit or a tax credit equal to 4 percent of social security payroll taxes and 2 percent of railroad retirement and self-employment taxes. The total revenue cost would be relatively minor, amounting to $0.9 billion in fiscal 1977 and $2.4 billion in fiscal 1978. Congress rejected the proposed tax credits and substituted an employment tax credit.

Under the congressional plan, employers receive a 50 percent tax credit for the first $4,200 in annual wages paid if the total payroll exceeds 102 percent of its level in the previous year. The 102 percent limit was imposed to reduce the extent to which the credit would have been paid for workers who would have been hired anyway in the absence of the tax subsidy. Unfortunately, the floor is unlikely to be very effective in accomplishing this goal. In many firms, payrolls would have increased more than 2 percent without the credit, in which case the subsidy becomes a windfall. On the other hand, the floor prevents slow-growing or declining firms from enjoying a subsidy that might have induced them to retain more workers. It is, in other words, a plan that benefits the strong competitor at the expense of the weak.

Moreover, the benefit is limited by a $100,000 ceiling, and the scheme is therefore unlikely to affect the marginal decisions of large growing firms; it ends up as a lump-sum windfall for such companies. Because the plan only subsidizes the first $4,200 of wages, it also encourages the substitution of low-wage, part-time, and temporary workers for more permanently employed, highly skilled labor. In sum, the plan leaves much to be desired. It has little impact on employment and serves mainly to complicate our tax laws.

Because Congress passed a higher standard deduction for joint returns than was recommended by Carter and because it substituted the employment tax credit for his business incentives, total receipts were lowered by $1.4 billion in fiscal 1977 and by $4.0 billion in 1978.

Public Service Employment. Carter proposed to increase the number of public service employment slots from 310,000 to 600,000 by the end of 1977 and to 725,000 during 1978. The cost is estimated at $0.7 billion in fiscal 1977 and $3.4 billion in 1978. Three important issues relate to the desirability of this program as a stimulative tool. How fast can people be hired by state and local governments? How many of them would have been hired in the absence of federal financial support? And how valuable is the output of such employment?

These three issues create important trade-offs for the designers of any public service employment program. The speed of hiring public service workers can be accelerated by minimizing restrictions on the type of person eligible for the program. However, with minimum restrictions the state and local governments are more likely to use the federal funds to hire people they would have hired anyway. This diminishes the program's impact on total employment, but it probably means that those hired will be used for tasks that are more valuable to the local community. If communities are forced to hire people they would not normally hire, it seems much more likely that the workers will be used inefficiently in the sense the local taxpayers will not place a high value on the services performed.

As is perhaps natural in a time of high unemployment, the Congress has placed more emphasis on the job creation impact of the program than on its economic efficiency. Since earlier studies of older, less restricted programs suggested that after two years, 60 to 90 percent of the public service employees were simply substitutes for employees who would have been hired anyway,[15] it was decided to target the CETA Title VI portion of the program more precisely when it was reauthorized during the last session of Congress. To reduce the substitution effect, half of all vacancies in Title VI are to be filled by the long-term unemployed, AFDC recipients, and unemployment compensation exhaustees. The new employees are to be used to produce specific public projects rather than to fill regular government jobs. Similar restrictions are placed on those hired under the expanded version of the program advocated by Carter. While such constraints will diminish the substitution of federal financing for state and local financing, it remains to be seen how they will affect the speed of hiring and the efficiency with which the people are used.

It should be noted that substitution is not all bad. If it results in federal deficits replacing state and local deficits, not much good or evil is done to the nation as a whole. If it results in lower state and local tax levels, the effect is more or less the same as that of a federal tax cut. At least when taxes are cut—whether federal, state, or local —one knows that people are able to use their increase in purchasing power for things that they desire. It is not clear that they get the same sort of benefit from the goods and services produced when public service employment actually results in someone new being hired by the state and local government.

As this is written, the program appears to be going more slowly than expected. The Office of Management and Budget blames a

---

[15] Alan Fechter, *Public Employment Programs* (Washington, D.C.: American Enterprise Institute, 1975).

delay in getting the authorization,[16] but the many restrictions placed on the program may also be playing a role.

Expanded Training and Youth Programs. Carter proposed an additional $0.3 billion in outlays for 1977 and $1.6 billion for 1978 for a great variety of training and employment programs focused on narrowly defined classes of unemployed such as youth and Vietnam era veterans. The amounts are sufficient to fund 200,000 full-time-equivalent job openings, but since most will be part-time jobs, the number of people directly affected will be considerably greater. The CBO expresses some worry that this program, on top of the public service jobs discussed above, may not be able to achieve its targets quickly.[17] If true, this is a rather serious indictment, because the long-run effectiveness of such programs has also been seriously questioned.[18]

Accelerated Public Works. Carter requested public works appropriations of $2 billion in each of 1977 and 1978, expecting outlays of $0.2 billion in the first year and $2.0 billion in the second year. These funds are for grants that will pay 100 percent of the cost of projects developed by state and local governments. Congress decided to appropriate the entire $4 billion in 1977. As a result of the congressional action, outlays were originally expected to rise to $0.4 billion in 1977 and to remain at $2.0 billion in 1978. The rest of the appropriation will be spent over the four or five years following 1978.

It is this long spendout period that makes public works a dubious short-run policy tool. Congress attempted to hasten the process by restricting eligibility to projects that can begin in six months, but there is no constraint on when they must be finished.

In analyzing the impact of such a program, one must again ask how many of the eligible projects would have been carried out by state and local governments if federal aid had not been available. Estimates of the effect of construction grants of this type suggest that the substitution effect may be substantial. Gramlich and Galper found no direct immediate impact of such grants on total state and local construction spending, and indicated that the impact was quite

---

[16] Office of Management and Budget, *Mid-Session Review of the 1978 Budget,* (Washington, D.C., 1977), p. 33.

[17] Congressional Budget Office, *Short-Run Measures to Stimulate the Economy,* p. 12.

[18] Orley Ashenfelter, "The Effect of Manpower Training on Earnings: Some Preliminary Results," *Proceedings of the Industrial Relations Research Association,* December 1974, pp. 252–60.

indirect and worked with a longtime lag.[19] However, certain provisions of the new legislation seek to minimize substitution. Communities must certify that the federally supported project has not started and that it is being delayed by a lack of local financial resources. It should also be noted that the Gramlich-Galper result is based on a statistical analysis of historical time series, and a program of this type may work differently in a period when depressed economic conditions are creating financial difficulties for lower levels of government. It seems particularly likely that the program will at least hasten the start of many projects, although it is more questionable whether it will hasten their completion. The CBO estimates that, overall, the substitution rate will be between zero and 25 percent: that is, between zero and 25 percent of the public works spending would have occurred in the absence of the program. The CBO estimates for the impact of a $5 billion program suggest that the $4 billion program passed by Congress will raise employment by 60,000 to 100,000 by the fourth quarter of 1978.

The CBO estimates do imply that the vast majority of the new projects would not have been chosen by state and local taxpayers if they had to pay the entire bill themselves. It is sometimes said that a great need for the projects is revealed by the fact that states and localities made proposals worth $24 billion in response to the $2 billion program initiated in October 1976. However, it must be remembered that the federal government is paying 100 percent of the cost, and free goods are always popular. Any project with a benefit-cost ratio greater than zero is, therefore, worthwhile to the state or locality, and the high demand for the projects is consequently not surprising.

Although it is far too early for a careful analysis, it appears that this program is also proceeding more slowly than expected and, from the experience with the October 1976 $2 billion program, it looks as the impact on employment will be much less than is suggested by the CBO estimates cited above. A *Wall Street Journal* article notes that in the projects financed in Baltimore, only 10 percent of those taking jobs were previously unemployed.[20] This may imply that the impact may show up more in increasing hours worked per already-employed worker rather than in generating new employment.

---

[19] Edward M. Gramlich and Harvey Galper, "State and Local Fiscal Behavior and Federal Grant Policy," *Brookings Papers on Economic Activity*, no. 1 (Washington, D.C., 1973), p. 31.

[20] "Public-Works Grants Help Baltimore a Bit, The Jobless Very Little," *Wall Street Journal* (July 21, 1977), p. 1.

Very little of the additional $4 billion appropriation will be spent in fiscal 1977, and it also seems safe to predict that there will be a spending shortfall in 1978.[21] At this early date, it is very hard to avoid the conclusion that grants for public works represent a highly ineffective countercyclical tool.

Countercyclical Revenue Sharing. Carter proposed to increase outlays on countercyclical revenue sharing and to extend the program through 1982. The revised program will provide for quarterly payments equal to $125 million, plus $30 million for each one-tenth of a percentage point that the national unemployment rate two quarters earlier exceeded 6.0 percent. Ford's budget would have allowed this program to expire at the end of 1977; the Carter extension and enlargement of the program will add $0.9 billion in outlays in 1977 and $1.6 billion in 1978. States and general-purpose local governments are eligible for the grants if the area they serve has an unemployment rate in excess of 4.5 percent. Their allocation is based on the amount by which their unemployment rate exceeds this figure and on the amount they receive from General Revenue Sharing. The program seeks to compensate lower levels of government for receipts lost because of the recession and thereby to forestall state and local spending cuts or tax increases.

The amount of fiscal duress suffered by state and local governments depends on the sensitivity of their tax system to changes in economic activity and on the extent to which economic activity in the state or locality fell below "normal" levels. Because normal levels of unemployment vary greatly from area to area, the use of a single standard unemployment rate of 4.5 percent for distributing funds is somewhat suspect, but probably unavoidable as a practical matter.

Where the funds are used to reduce deficits or increase cash balances, there will be little or no impact on economic activity. Where they forestall spending cuts or tax increases, the effects are roughly comparable to increased federal spending or tax cuts.

The CBO analysis of this program stresses the difficulty of making impact estimates, but on the basis of their estimate for slightly different additions to the program, it appears as though their model would estimate an increase in employment from 50,000 to 75,000 in the last quarter of 1978.[22]

---

[21] Office of Management and Budget, *Mid-Session Review*, pp. 31–32.
[22] Congressional Budget Office, *Short-Run Measures*, pp. 29–35.

Conclusions

No area of economics has received as much critical reexamination in the last ten years as the effect of government fiscal and monetary policy on aggregate economic activity. In the face of this intellectual turmoil, Carter and his advisers have chosen to base their approach to stabilization policy on the Keynesian precepts popular in the early 1960s. To the extent that there are uncertainties regarding the wisdom of this strategy, they probably played a role in limiting the size of the program and in the decision to withdraw the rebate. Whether the overall strategy was a wise one will be debated vigorously by economists in the future, but this preliminary analysis suggests that history is unlikely to look favorably on the stimulus package.

The slowdown in the economy in the last part of 1976, which inspired the proposals, proved to be temporary, and the severe winter of 1976–1977 had little lasting influence on economic activity. Long before the stimulus package had any impact, the economy began to grow vigorously. This recovery probably makes it fortuitous that the public works and public service employment programs are slow getting off the ground, and if the increased spending is required in 1978 and in later years, when it will actually occur, it will be a matter of pure luck. Even if such spending turns out to be needed, one has to expect that many inefficient projects will be created by the program because of the fact that state and local governments are being handed free goods with little insurance that they will be used for the best projects possible.

Although the above analysis is highly preliminary, two lessons seem to emerge. First is the oft-cited danger of reacting too quickly to temporary fluctuations in economic activity. The temporary slowdown in late 1976 proved too short-lived to be affected by changes in government policy. As a recovery proceeds, it cannot be expected to proceed smoothly. There almost certainly will be temporary slowdowns during any economic expansion. A policy maker who reacts too quickly to such slowdowns may end up destabilizing the economy.

Second, temporary spending programs are too unwieldy for "fine," or even "coarse," tuning. Keynesian models suggest that one gets more "bang for the buck" from spending increases than from tax reductions, but even if this is true it should be a minor consideration in designing a stimulus program. The time lag in implementing spending programs is likely to be very long, and efforts to shorten this lag are very likely to make the programs more inefficient. At least with a tax cut, one knows that the recipients will spend for the goods and services that they desire. It is not clear that they get what they want from a hastily implemented spending program.

Permanent tax reductions are also likely to have salutary effects on the private supply of goods and services by reducing disincentives. The size of this response is a matter of great dispute and it is not recorded in the typical Keynesian model. But to the extent it exists, tax cuts will be less inflationary than spending increases of the type contained in the Carter stimulus package. While it is probably too much to hope that politicians will eschew fiscal "fine tuning" in the future, it is to be hoped that next time, permanent tax cuts will receive much more serious consideration.

PART TWO
SELECTED BUDGET ISSUES

7
SOCIAL SECURITY

The social security system directly affects more Americans than any other federal program. At the end of fiscal 1976, retirement and survivors' benefits were paid to 27.5 million persons, and disability benefits to 4.4 million. During fiscal 1976, 517 million received aid from hospital insurance and 14.0 million from the special medical insurance program. More important, virtually the entire private sector labor force and a large proportion of public sector employees have, at some time in their working career, participated in the system and earned rights to future benefits. In the Old Age and Survivors Insurance (OASI) part of the system, some vitally important budget choices will have to be made in the near future. Indeed, these decisions will probably be much more important to the long-run budget outlook than any other set of decisions discussed in this volume.

In calendar 1956, outlays under the OASI system mounted to $5.7 billion or 1.4 percent of GNP. Twenty years later, in 1976, outlays had grown to $65.7 billion or to 3.9 percent of GNP. Payments under the disability insurance program, which did not begin until 1957, included another $9.9 billion in outlays in 1976, 0.6 percent of GNP. For reasons discussed below, the burden of OASI can be expected to grow relative to GNP in the long run, although not at the rate experienced over the last twenty years.

The rise in the ratio of social security outlays to GNP has been entirely financed by major increases in the social security payroll tax. In 1956, this tax constituted less than 8 percent of federal revenues. Twenty years later, it provided more than one-quarter of revenues and has since 1967 been a more important part of the total tax burden than the corporate tax. For the vast majority of families earning less than $10,000, the payroll tax is now more important than the personal income tax.

The OASI system is run on a pay-as-you-go basis. That is, the bulk of its resources are collected from the payroll tax and are immediately paid out to retirees, their dependent spouses, and survivors of deceased workers. There is a trust fund, but it covers only a tiny proportion of the future liability of the system. Its function is to act as a cushion, absorbing funds when payroll tax receipts exceed benefit payments and supplying funds when there is a shortfall. The total payroll tax rate, including hospital insurance, is currently 11.7 per cent. Half is paid by employers and half by employees on a maximum wage base, which was $15,300 in 1976. The base is automatically raised from year to year by an amount equal to the percentage increase in average covered wages. The growth of the total amount of financial resources available to the system depends on the growth in the number of taxpaying workers, the growth in their wages, and on the rate of increase in the tax rate that they pay. The resulting pool of financial resources is shared among the population of beneficiaries.

The late 1960s and early 1970s might be called the "glory days" of the OASI system. Tax receipts grew rapidly because of the rapidly growing labor force which resulted from the relatively high birth rates in the 1940s and 1950s. An expansion of coverage combined with sustained rapid economic growth and a steadily rising tax rate added to the resources of the system in the 1960s. This relative abundance allowed a 70 percent across-the-board cumulative increase in individual benefits in the six-year period 1967 through 1972.

As a result, individuals retiring in the late 1960s received a relatively high rate of return on taxes paid. Using methods that understate the return slightly, Freiden, Leimer, and Hoffman of the Social Security Administration calculate that the average internal rate of return to the single worker retiring between 1967 and 1970 was about 15 percent per year.[1] For reasons discussed below, the rate of return can be expected to erode in the future. As this occurs, it will be interesting to see whether the system retains its current high level of popularity.

The basic benefit structure of OASI has many characteristics of a compulsory contributory pension program. A worker is fully

---

[1] U.S. Department of Health, Education, and Welfare, Social Security Administration, "Internal Rate of Return to Retired Worker-Only Beneficiaries under Social Security, 1967–70," *Studies in Income Distribution*, 77-11776.

insured if payroll taxes have been paid on wage earnings of at least $50 or on self-employed earnings of $100 in forty quarters of his working life.[2] Benefits depend on the so-called primary insurance amount (PIA), which is related in turn to the worker's average monthly earnings (AME) using a complicated formula. In general, the AME is based on total covered earnings between 1950 and age 62 divided by the number of months since 1950, with the lowest five years of earnings omitted.

While the eligibility requirements and the relationships between benefit size and covered earnings make social security similar to a normal private retirement system, the social security system also has characteristics that significantly differentiate it from a pure contributory system. In particular, the relationship between earnings and benefits is a weak one. For example, benefits are greatly affected by the marital circumstances of the beneficiary. If a male worker aged 65 retires with a dependent spouse who is also 65, the benefit is 150 percent of the PIA. In addition, the ratio of the PIA to the AME declines as the AME rises, and there is a relatively high minimum benefit—$107 per month in early 1977. It is sometimes said that this benefit structure tends to redistribute income in a progressive manner. However, the AME is based only on covered earnings, and therefore, the structure can also favor high-income earners who worked part of their career in a noncovered sector with its own pension system, such as the federal government.

The relationship in 1976 between the PIA and the AME can be approximated by the following formula. The PIA equals:

137.77% of the first $110 of AME
50.11% of the next $290
46.85% of the next $150
55.04% of the next $100
30.61% of the next $100
25.51% of the next $250
22.98% of the next $175
21.28% of the next $100

This tabulation covers workers with AMEs up to $1,275 per month or $15,300 per year, the 1976 maximum covered wage base. Since the maximum covered wage base was much lower in the past than currently, no worker retiring in the last half of 1976 could have had

---

[2] For persons who reached age 21 prior to 1950 the requirement is less stringent. One-quarter of coverage is required for every year between 1951 and the year in which the worker reached retirement age.

an AME this high. The maximum possible monthly benefit for a single worker retiring in the last half of 1976 is $387; that is, no recent retiree can be above the fourth bracket level in the above table.

Short-Run Problem

Largely because of the 1974–1975 recession and the long time it is taking to again attain low unemployment rates, outlays for both the OASI and disability (DI) systems significantly exceed receipts. This is exacerbated by the fact that outlays are being increased rapidly by the high rate of inflation which persists despite the economy's operating at far less than full capacity. As a result, the trust funds are being depleted. Even given highly optimistic assumptions about future economic conditions, it is likely that the disability trust fund will be depleted before 1980, and the old age and survivors trust fund will evaporate before 1985. It should hastily be emphasized that this will not put anyone's benefits in jeopardy. As noted earlier, the system is fundamentally on a pay-as-you-go basis, the deficit is small relative to total benefits, and the role of the trust funds is not inherently very important. However, the depletion of the trust funds is a symptom of the fact that social security is now more expensive relative to our economic resources than earlier expected, and this point *is* of significant importance.

If the sole source of this difficulty were the 1974–1975 recession and the greater than expected inflation, the trust funds could borrow while they are in deficit and repay when the economy returned to relative price stability and full employment. Unfortunately, by the time this occurs, even under the most optimistic economic assumptions the long-run problems discussed below begin to have a significant impact, and there is little hope of ever making up the deficit under current social security tax and benefit law. In this sense, the distinction between short- and long-run problems is somewhat artificial.

President Ford set forth proposals for dealing with the short-run financing problem in his budgets for 1977 and 1978. President Carter made his proposals in May 1977. The solutions of the two presidents differ markedly in their underlying philosophy. Ford took the very direct approach of raising the payroll tax rate sufficiently to prevent the trust funds from declining much further relative to outlays. He advocated a 0.2 percentage point increase in the OASDI tax rate in 1978, in addition to the 0.4 percentage point increase already scheduled for the hospital insurance (HI) tax. Further increases of 0.6 and 0.3 percentage points were recommended for 1979 and 1980.

Given a scheduled HI increase of 0.5 percentage points in 1981, the implied total social security tax for that year under the Ford proposal is 13.7 percent, compared with a 1977 rate of 11.7 percent.

President Carter went to extreme lengths to avoid an immediate rate increase in the short run, although he did not avoid an increase in the long run. His short-run package is as follows.

- He proposes general revenue payments to the OASDI trust funds in an amount equal to the amount by which payroll tax receipts fall short of the level that would be generated with the national unemployment rate of 6 percent.
- He requires employers to pay payroll taxes on their entire payroll instead of only on individual earnings up to the maximum wage base, which is currently $16,500.
- He raises the tax rate on the self-employed to one and a half times the employee tax rate. This would raise the self-employed tax rate to 7.5 percent in 1979.
- He shifts a portion of the HI tax increases that are scheduled in current law for 1978 and 1981 to the OASDI trust funds.
- Beginning in 1979 and in each alternative year through 1985, the maximum employee wage base is raised $600, in addition to the automatic increases set by current law.
- In earlier law, men had to prove that they were dependent on their wives in order to claim dependency benefits, whereas women were presumed to be dependent on their husbands. The Supreme Court ruled that this was sex discrimination and the dependency test was eliminated for men. Carter proposes a new dependency test for both spouses. Under his plan, only the spouse with lower income over the preceding three-year period can claim to be dependent.

The proposal for using general revenue financing is probably the most controversial part of the package. Many oppose this step for fear that it will erode the remaining vestiges of the contributory philosophy of the social security system. This is thought to encourage the enhancement of the system's welfare components, which will diminish the system's popular support. Carter attempted to dilute the force of this criticism by limiting the extent of general revenue financing to the amount provided by a strict formula related to the unemployment rate. He also made the provision temporary and subject to renewal only if advocated by the Social Security Advisory Commission Report due at the end of 1978.

Carter chose to tax employers on their whole payroll instead of advocating larger wage base increases for employers and employees because the latter option would have increased future retirement benefits and would, thereby, increase the economic burden imposed by the system. Many argue that this imposes a disproportionate share of the social security burden on business. On the other hand, a number of economists say that the business sector successfully shifts payroll taxes back to employees either by slowing the growth in before-tax wages or by increasing the prices of everything that employees buy. If such shifting occurs, employees end up with a higher tax burden without any increased benefits to show for it. Of course, such a reduction in rates of return to social security payments is inevitable one way or another given the economic and demographic problems besetting the system.

It should also be noted that even if the employer's tax burden is eventually shifted to the worker, the process of shifting can be extremely painful to the business sector in the short run. For example, in order to shift the burden by charging higher prices, business may have to reduce production and employment. The Federal Reserve System can mitigate the problem by printing enough money to finance the ensuing inflation, but some businesses will be afflicted by the new tax burden more than others and a painful adjustment process cannot be entirely avoided.

The Carter-proposed increase in the tax rate on the self-employed to its historic level of one and a half times the employee tax should not be controversial, although it will obviously be opposed by those who have to pay the tax increase. But if one assumes that employees end up paying the employer share of the payroll tax because it lowers wages, the self-employed get a very favorable deal from social security even at the new higher tax rate.[3]

The Carter-proposed shift of HI revenues to OASDI is a bit more dubious. The administration argues that Medicare can afford this revenue loss because their proposal to control the prices of medical services (see chapter 9) will result in large savings. At the time of writing, there is considerable uncertainty whether the administration price control proposals will be adopted by Congress, but even if they are, past experiments with price controls have not been characterized by overwhelming success. The Carter proposal may, therefore, just be shifting the deficit of the OASDI trust funds to HI,

---

[3] It should be noted that the treatment of the self-employed is not quite as generous as it seems at first sight. Employees do not pay income tax on the employer share of the payroll tax, whereas the self-employed must pay income taxes on their entire payroll tax payment.

which may then require future HI payroll tax increases or general revenue financing. While the latter would be disturbing in that it may remove some financial discipline on the HI program, it should be noted that the argument against general revenue financing for HI is not quite as compelling as the argument against it for OASDI. Benefits under the HI program have never borne much relationship to taxes paid, other than in the determination of eligibility, and there is thus virtually no contributory philosophy to be sacrificed.

Carter's proposed increase in the taxable wage base over the period 1979–1985 may be criticized because it raises future benefit entitlements and so raises the future size of social security relative to GNP. Given the Carter benefit indexing plan (see below), the benefits purchased by these wage-base increases are, however, likely to be very low, and while the future ratio of social security benefits to GNP rises, wage-base increases do raise trust fund revenues more than they raise eventual outlays.

Carter's last proposal to impose a sex-neutral dependency test should be noncontroversial, but it will obviously be opposed mightily by those who lose benefits as a result of its imposition.

Carter obviously resorted to a highly complex social security financing plan solely to avoid the sort of tax rate increases advocated by President Ford. He did, however, continue to rely heavily on payroll taxes by using employee-employer wage base increases rather than tax rate increases in order to make up the short-run social security deficit. Of the total $72.1 billion in savings and increased taxes implied by the Carter plan for the period 1977–1982, only $14.1 billion comes from general-revenue financing.

Some might argue that Carter should have relied even less on payroll tax increases because payroll taxes raise the cost of labor, thus raising prices and increasing unemployment. This sort of criticism is, of course, only valid if employers are not able to shift the tax burden fairly rapidly to the laborer by providing lesser wage increases than would otherwise occur.

With regard to the payroll tax itself, the main dispute between Ford and Carter is, given a decision to raise the payroll tax, is it better to raise the wage base or the tax rate? Although Carter does provide for a rate increase in the long run, he avoids one immediately on the grounds that a rate increase would heighten the regressive nature of the payroll tax.

But is this a legitimate concern? There are a number of arguments to the contrary. First, there is absolutely no reason that every tax in our system has to be progressive. Income redistribution by government is the result of the simultaneous impact of our whole tax and transfer system. If a more regressive tax for some reason serves the purposes of the social security system, it can easily be offset by a more progressive income tax structure. For example, the earned income credit, first passed in 1975, represents a major effort to offset the distributional effects of the payroll tax. One's attitude to such efforts can of course vary depending on how progressive one feels that the whole tax-transfer system should be, and President Ford chose to oppose the earned income credit.

Second, because of explicit earmarking, there is a strong argument that the social security tax and benefit structure should be considered as a package. The whole package is clearly progressive on balance, in the sense that low-income workers generally receive a higher rate of return on payroll tax payments than do high-income workers. Third, the regressive relationship between an individual's earnings and the payroll tax is not very relevant to judging regressivity as it is usually measured even if the payroll tax is examined in isolation. Our income tax system generally regards the family as the taxpaying unit, and the tax burden is measured relative to total income, not just relative to wage earnings.

When viewed in this light, the payroll tax is not very regressive at all. At low levels of income, families tend to receive a lot of transfer payments and retirement income that are not subject to the payroll tax. Therefore, on average, the payroll tax burden is quite low relative to total income, although there can be significant differences in the burden from family to family. At the other end of the income distribution, many of those families with total earnings above the wage base attain high income levels because more than one member of the family works.

Table 15 illustrates the average federal income tax rate and employee's share of the payroll tax rate paid by different income groups. (As already noted, many analysts believe that employees also pay the employer's share of the payroll tax in that it results in lower wages, but because there is still considerable uncertainty regarding the matter, the employer's share is not shown.) The payroll tax is actually progressive over the bottom four quintiles of the income distribution and does not become regressive until the highest quintile. To the extent that the wage base is increased, the burden falls entirely on the top 40 percent of the income distribution unless, of course, some part of wage base increases are shifted forward in the form of higher prices, in which case the whole population suffers to some degree. Tax rate increases affect the whole working popula-

Table 15

ESTIMATED OASDHI TAXES AND FEDERAL INCOME TAXES
PAID AS A PERCENTAGE OF FAMILY INCOME FOR
EACH INCOME QUINTILE OF FAMILIES, 1976
(percent distribution)

Quintiles	Total Family Income, 1976[a]	Federal Income Taxes	OASDHI Taxes[b]
Lowest (under $5,669)	100.0	2.3	2.4
Second ($5,676–$9,853)	100.0	4.1	3.5
Third ($9,854–$14,678)	100.0	8.1	4.4
Fourth ($14,679–$21,539)	100.0	11.3	4.6
Highest ($21,540 and over)	100.0	17.1	3.6
All families	100.0	12.1	3.9

[a] Unrelated individuals are counted as families. Income includes an estimate of capital gains as well as wages and salaries, self-employment income, interest, dividends, rent, social security, government and private pension, public assistance, veterans' benefits, workmen's compensation, unemployment compensation, alimony, and income from miscellaneous sources.
[b] Employee's share.
Source: Congressional Budget Office, *Financing Social Security: Issues for the Short and Long Term*, p. 10.

tion, but the largest share of the burden would appear to fall on the third and fourth quintiles of the income distribution.

Of course, within each quintile of the entire income distribution, different individuals would be affected very differently by a tax rate increase, depending on whether they were working in a covered occupation. The average payroll tax burden is low in the bottom quintiles because they contain so much of the population that is not working. In particular, retired elderly persons constitute a very large share of the lowest quintile. If only the working population is considered, the payroll tax burden is roughly proportional through the bottom four quintiles, and the working poor are hard hit by an increase in the payroll tax rate. But the burden should not be exaggerated. A person earning wages of $5,000 per year would pay extra employee taxes of about $0.50 per week under the Ford proposal. If it is assumed that this worker also "pays" the employer share, the increased burden would be slightly more than $1 per week. If the worker has dependents, the amount received from the 1975 earned income credit was almost $6 per week. This could easily be increased if it were deemed desirable to offset the increased payroll tax burden, although as already noted this offset was opposed by President Ford. He favored the elimination of the earned income credit.

There are, of course, options for dealing with the short-run financing problem that differ from the solutions proposed by Ford and Carter. For example, there has been some discussion of creating a new earmarked tax whose proceeds would be paid into the OASDI trust fund. An earmarked tax is said to be preferable to general revenue financing because the fact of earmarking may impose more discipline on future outlays. However, considerable discipline is also imposed by Carter's strict formula for limiting the extent of general revenue financing. Various types of earmarked sales or value added taxes have been mentioned as substitutes for general revenue financing. However, given the above discussion of the distributional implications of the payroll tax, it is hard to imagine any sales tax that would have a distributional impact clearly superior to that of a payroll tax rate increase.

Long-Run Problems

The social security system faces two major problems in the longer run: demographic trends have turned against the system as birth rates have fallen, and current law indexes future social security benefits in a way that overcompensates for inflation. If this flaw is not corrected, retirement benefits will eventually become extremely generous and the economic burden imposed by the system will grow accordingly.

Demographic Trends. The surge in fertility rates in the 1940s and 1950s and the consequent impact on labor force growth in the late 1960s and early 1970s was very favorable to the financial health of the social security system in that it significantly curbed the growth in the ratio of the beneficiary to the taxpaying population. (These favorable developments have, to some degree, been offset by earlier retirements and increased coverage.) This "baby boom" appears to have been a short-run anomaly that briefly interrupted the longer downward trend in fertility rates that has persisted in this nation for as long as records have been maintained. By 1975, the fertility rate (number of births per woman) had fallen to 1.8, far below the postwar peak of 3.7 in 1957 and even significantly below the level of 2.1 necessary to maintain a constant population in the absence of immigration.

This plunge in fertility rates during the 1960s and early 1970s guarantees a steady increase over the next two decades in the percentage of the population consisting of persons 65 or over. In 1950 that percentage was 8.1, by 1974 it was 10.3, and by 1995 it will be close to 12 percent. The system will get a brief respite around the turn of the century when the members of the baby trough of the Great Depression retire, but assuming that a dramatic rise in birth rates does not occur very quickly, the burden implied by social security will rise rapidly after that time when those born during the baby boom retire.[4]

The severity of the burden in the first half of the twenty-first century will, of course, be affected by fertility rates between now and then. For example, if the fertility rate is at 1.7 in 1985 and remains constant from then on, the ratio of the 65 and over to the 20- to 64-year-old population will be 19.0 percent in 1985 and 36.0 percent in 2050. If the trend in fertility rates reverses and rises to 2.3 in 1985 and remains constant thereafter, the ratio in 2050 will be 25.5 percent, still higher than the 19.0 percent in 1985.

While any definite statement regarding future fertility rates is dangerous, the above data suggest that it would take a revolution in past trends to avoid dramatic increases in the future ratio of the retired to working population. The rise in this ratio combined with the indexing problem discussed below are the two most important factors increasing the future burden to be imposed by social security.

Some argue that while demographic trends will increase the burden of social security, the burden will become more affordable if birth rates remain low because child-rearing costs will be reduced. This theory has merit, but it also implies that the worst possible outcome would be a surge in fertility rates about the turn of the century—too late to add to the labor force that will have to finance the retirement of the baby boom of the 1940s and 1950s, but early enough to increase child-rearing expenses at a time when retirement costs also begin to soar.

There are reforms which could significantly affect the ratio of

---

[4] Immigration is now responsible for a larger part of our population growth. Increased immigration of younger persons can ease the problems of the system. This analysis, however, accepts the immigration estimates implicit in the social security actuary's population forecasts.

the retired to the taxpaying population. For example, the retirement age could be increased, but this would have to be done very gradually to avoid upsetting the retirement plans of those who are near retirement. A long time period is also required to allow the adjustment of private pension plans to social security.

The taxpaying population could be increased by bringing federal and state and local workers into the social security system. At first their tax payments would significantly exceed benefit payments, but of course, in the very long run, they would begin to earn full benefits. It would also be a complex and politically controversial matter to design a supplementary federal retirement system that was equitable without imposing major extra costs.

Indexing Benefits. Prior to 1972, benefits were not indexed to the rate of inflation. However, Congress periodically passed benefit increases that had the effect over the long run of more than compensating retirees for the increases in the cost of living. In 1972 Congress decided to index the system, so that benefits would automatically keep pace with the standard of living. Unfortunately, Congress overdid it by choosing an indexing method that overcompensated for price increases.[5]

To understand the indexing problem, it is useful to repeat the benefit schedules prescribed by current law. In 1976 it provided a PIA of:

137.77% of the first $110 of AME
50.11% of the next $290
46.85% of the next $150
55.04% of the next $100
30.61% of the next $100
25.51% of the next $250
22.98% of the next $175
21.28% of the next $100

Every year, the percentages shown at the left are increased in June by the amount that the consumer price index (CPI) rises between the first quarter of the preceding year and the first quarter of the current year. For example, the CPI rose by 5.9 percent between the first quarter of 1976 and the first quarter of 1977. In 1976 single retirees

---

[5] For a more detailed analysis of the indexing problem, see Colin D. Campbell, *Over-Indexed Benefits: The Decoupling Proposals for Social Security* (Washington, D.C.: American Enterprise Institute, 1976); and J. W. Van Gorkom, *Social Security: The Long Run Deficit* (Washington, D.C.: American Enterprise Institute, 1976).

were entitled to 137.77 percent of the first $110 of AME, and therefore, for 1977, this percentage will be increased 5.9 percent, or to 145.90 percent. All the other percentages will be increased by the same percentage amount. This change in the benefit structure increases the benefit level that can be expected by all those currently working. At the same time, all those currently retired receive the same percentage increase in their benefits.

This indexing method implies that individuals retiring in successive years with the same money AME will receive the same real benefit. For example, a 1976, single, 65-year-old retiree with an AME of $110 will received $152 per month, while a 1977 retiree with exactly the same AME will receive $161 per month—an amount 5.9 percent higher because of the 5.9 percent CPI adjustment. But on average, one would expect inflation to increase wages and therefore to increase AMEs. An increased AME also entitles a retiree to a higher benefit. Thus, the current indexing method results in people's receiving two benefits from inflation—one resulting from an increase in the benefit as a percentage of a given money AME and one resulting from the increase in AMEs resulting from inflation. For this reason, it is often said that the current system is "double indexed." The result is overcompensation for inflation and a continued increase in the real benefits provided by the system.

It is particularly disturbing that the rate of increase in real benefits is directly related to the rate of inflation, that is, a higher inflation rate implies a higher rate of growth of real benefits—an outcome that makes very little sense. Moreover, inflation rates that are modest compared with those of the last five years imply that under present law social security benefits will become extraordinarily generous in the twenty-first century. For example, if the rate of growth of real wages is 1.25 percent and the inflation rate is 5 percent, a worker retiring with a spouse aged 65 would in the year 2000 receive social security benefits equal to 89 percent of earnings in the year preceding retirement if the median covered wage was earned over his or her career. Given that social security benefits are not taxed, it is very likely that after-tax income would rise after retirement. In addition, such a worker is very likely to have rights to a private pension which would further enhance the couples' standard of living.

As time goes on, the system becomes even more generous at a rapid rate. By the year of 2025, a similar couple would receive tax-free social security benefits equal to 121 percent of their gross preretirement earnings. By 2050 the ratio rises to 145 percent!

There is unanimous agreement that such benefits are too generous. There is less agreement regarding the appropriate solution to the problem. While double indexing is often considered to represent a "technical flaw" in the design of the 1972 law, the problem cannot be corrected by a simple technical amendment. We have to decide on what to put in its place, and this choice involves profound value judgments that go to the core of the basic philosophy underlying the social security system. Put another way, indexing is only a mechanical device for implementing value judgments. Moreover, the choice of an index method must be made with due consideration to the economic burden that will be imposed on future generations by various options, and predictions of that burden are extremely sensitive to the choice of assumptions regarding future economic growth and birth rates.

There is an infinite number of options available for dealing with the double indexing problem. One obvious approach, which has no popular support whatsoever, would be to drop indexing and return to the situation prevailing before 1972. Without indexing and without offsetting discretionary actions by Congress, a nonindexed system would rapidly become less generous and, therefore, less costly. The situation would be the exact opposite of that created by our nonindexed income tax law. Under a given, nonindexed income tax law, inflation and real growth inexorably push taxpayers into higher and higher tax brackets, thus increasing the tax burden. Under constant social security tax law, inflation and real growth raise the earnings of the working population, thus raising their eventual AME and pushing them into higher benefit brackets where the ratio of benefits to the AME is lower. At the same time the real standard of living of those already retired would be eroded by inflation.

However, in the twenty years prior to 1972, Congress more than compensated for the erosion of benefits with periodic increases in the ratio of the PIA to AME in the benefit schedule and by increasing the benefits for those already retired. While benefits were not increased every year, the erosion in their real value was never allowed to go on very long and, of course, over much of the period there was very little inflation to offset.

There is an important difference between the periodic discretionary benefit increases occurring prior to 1972 and the automatic adjustment system implemented in that year. The typical benefit increase prior to 1972 provided equal increases in the prospective benefits of the working population and in the pensions of those already retired. As a result, those already retired received benefit increases that more than compensated for inflation, actually improving their standard of living. The double indexing approach adopted in 1972 increases the prospective real benefits to the working population, but once a person retires, benefits are held constant in real terms. As a result, the retiree does not share in any growth in living standards after retirement and, consequently, his or her economic status declines relative to that of the working population and new retirees unless Congress provides discretionary benefit increases on top of the automatic cost of living increases.

Since discretionary increases are rare now that the system is indexed, there has been a significant implicit change in the philosophy of the system. Prior to 1972, those already retired continued to share in the real growth of the nation. Since 1972, they have not. This important change in philosophy has received very little attention.[6]

Although the option of dropping indexing is quite unlikely to receive any political support, it may be useful to say a few quixotic words in its favor. The future burden imposed by any indexed system is quite uncertain and depends on future birth rates, productivity increases, and labor force participation. The future need for social security depends on the evolution of the private pension and the welfare systems. Since both costs and needs are impossible to predict with any degree of accuracy, there would appear to be some merit in making constant discretionary adjustments to the system in response to changing conditions, rather than to rely on an automatically adjusted system whose growth depends on factors that are essentially beyond our control. It is clearly easier to take discretionary actions to enhance the generosity of a system that is growing "too slowly" than it is to take discretionary actions to slow down a system that is automatically growing "too fast." It is also easier to make structural changes that increase the equity of the system if it is growing slowly, because any politically feasible structural changes are sure to involve discretionary increases in average benefits.

There is, of course, a large number of arguments in favor of indexing. The first is disturbing because it depends on the notion that Congress is inherently irresponsible. There is a fear that periodic discretionary increases are likely to be too large and to occur immediately before elections in order to attract the support of the politically powerful elderly population. It is true that the behavior of Congress

---

[6] The development of criteria for judging the equity of social security is a highly complex matter which is not fully explored in this chapter. For a detailed discussion, see D. R. Leimer, R. Hoffman, and A. Freiden, "A Framework for Analyzing the Equity of the Social Security Benefit Structure," U.S. Department of Health, Education and Welfare, Social Security Administration, *Studies in Income Distribution*, forthcoming.

between 1967 and 1972 was not reassuring when it provided a 70 per cent increase in benefits, but, as already noted, all the economic and demographic conditions were highly favorable at that time and the current, more sobering economic and demographic outlook might impose more stringent constraints on congressional action.

A very different argument for indexing involves the notion that Congress would act too slowly rather than be too generous. Because of its ponderous procedures, Congress often has difficulty acting quickly, and there would be periods during which real benefits would erode, but this is only a serious problem during periods of rapid inflation. A more persuasive argument for indexing is that, if done correctly, it may make an individual's future benefits relative to his lifetime standard of living more predictable, which is a major advantage given that individuals must plan for their retirement over a long time horizon. Ironically, the present indexing system does not have a predictable result since the real value of future benefits is enormously sensitive to the vagaries of the inflation rate.

Instead of abandoning indexing altogether, benefits might be indexed to the CPI in order to maintain their real value after a person retires, but the benefit schedule might be left unindexed. Inflation and real growth would then constantly erode the prospective replacement rates for the working population and Congress would have to make periodic adjustments to offset this erosion. This allows the adjustment of future social security costs to changing economic and demographic conditions, but protects the already-retired from erosions in their living standards. It does, however, subject prospective pensions to considerable uncertainty and therefore makes retirement planning difficult.

Although the options of completely or partially abandoning indexing are not without advantages, it is unlikely that they will be considered seriously as potential substitutes for the current double indexed system. The two options that have attracted most attention both result in a completely indexed system. One of these options was recommended in 1976 by a panel of experts organized by the Congressional Reference Service at the request of Congress. It will henceforth be called the Hsiao option after the chairman of the panel. The other was recommended by the 1974 Social Security Advisory Committee and was adopted by Ford in his 1976 recommendations to the Congress. Carter adopted exactly the same approach in his May 1977 recommendations. It will henceforth be called the Carter option. Both the Hsiao and Carter options retain the current approach for indexing the benefits of those already retired. That is to say, the money value of their benefits would be increased at the same rate as the inflation rate as measured by the CPI. However, they take different approaches to indexing the benefit schedule and therefore have very different implications for the size of benefits to be received by the population that is currently working (and for those not yet in the labor force assuming that the indexing law remains constant for that long).

The Hsiao approach implies average benefits that grow at a slightly slower rate than the Carter benefits, and is therefore very much less costly in the long run. Under reasonable economic and demographic assumptions, the Hsiao cost saving over the next seventy-five years has a present value of about $500 billion. The philosophy underlying the Hsiao approach is that those retiring at different times with the same lifetime real covered income should receive the same real benefits. For example, a person retiring in 1990 whose average annual income over his or her lifetime was $8,000 in 1976 dollars would, under the Hsiao proposal, get exactly the same benefit as the person who retired ten years earlier or in 1980 with the same average annual lifetime income.

Similarly, a person retiring with a real income of $10,000 in 1990 would get exactly the same real benefit as a person retiring in 1980 with the same real income. But because the social security benefit schedule is progressive, the ratio of benefits to income is lower for the $10,000 person in both years than it is for the $8,000 person. Economic growth will cause the higher income retirees to become relatively more numerous over time, and therefore the average ratio of benefits to income for all retirees will decline between 1980 and 1990. Consequently, it is often said that the Hsiao proposal implies a declining replacement rate (the ratio of benefits to pre-retirement earnings). This does not imply that replacement rates or average benefits decline for anyone at a given living standard. As already explained, real benefits are held constant at each level of real income. Average real benefits grow as average real income grows, but because the benefit structure is progressive, average benefits grow slightly more slowly than average living standards. Hence, the average replacement rate declines, with its rate of decline directly dependent on the rate of economic growth. If for some reason the economy does not grow, the Hsiao option implies a constant average ratio of benefits to lifetime covered income.

In contrast, the Carter proposal seeks to counteract the dampening effect of real growth on the average ratio of benefits to lifetime earnings. It indexes so that people retiring at different times but at the same place in the relative income scale receive the same ratio of benefits to average earnings. For example, assume that a person retiring in 1990 with $8,000 in 1976 dollars was at the same relative position in the wage distribution as a person retiring in 1980 with $6,563. Under the Carter proposals, both would receive the same ratio of benefits to earnings. To achieve this result the ratio has to be gradually increased at each absolute level of real earnings. In other words, the Carter proposal implies that individuals retiring in 1990 with real earnings of $6,563 would receive more benefits than individuals retiring in 1980 with exactly the same average level of real income.

In summary, the difference between the Hsiao and Carter goals can be put this way. Hsiao wants to insure that those attaining a certain absolute living standard will receive the same ratio of benefits to earnings in the future as they do currently. Carter wants to insure that those attaining a certain relative position in the earnings distribution will receive the same ratio of benefits to earnings in the future as they do currently. Hence, under the Carter proposal a person earning the median income throughout his or her career and retiring in 1990 would receive the same ratio of benefits to earnings as the person retiring in 1980. The same principle would apply to those in each quintile of earnings.

If birth and death rates had remained constant for several generations, the Carter proposal would imply that retirement benefits would remain a constant share of GNP. The Hsiao proposal would imply that the ratio of social security benefits to GNP would gradually decline as living standards improve. However, the decline in birth rates since the late 1950s implies that the ratio of the retired to working population will rise significantly in the early twenty-first century. As a result, both proposals imply that the ratio of benefits to GNP rises, but the rise implied by the Hsiao proposal is very much less than that implied by the Carter proposal. Table 16 illustrates the future costs of the two proposals relative to projections of covered wages, comparing them with the implications of current law and with the OASDI tax rate. The projections assume a 4 percent inflation rate, a 1.75 percent annual rate of growth in real wages, and a fertility rate of 1.9. Unlike the current double indexed system, the costs of the Hsiao and Carter proposals are not highly sensitive to the inflation rate. They are, however, sensitive to assumptions regarding real growth and fertility rates.

One cannot assess the relative desirability of the Hsiao versus the Carter proposals without examining the fundamental philosophy

Table 16

PROJECTED OASDI BENEFITS AS A PERCENTAGE OF TAXABLE EARNINGS UNDER CURRENT LAW AND HSIAO AND CARTER PROPOSALS

Year	Current Law	Carter Proposal	Hsiao Proposal	OASDI Tax Rate (current law)
1976	10.8	10.8	10.8	9.9
1980	10.7	10.7	10.6	9.9
1990	12.1	11.8	10.5	9.9
2000	13.4	12.4	10.0	9.9
2010	16.0	13.4	10.0	9.9
2020	21.3	16.5	11.5	11.9
2030	26.0	18.9	12.5	11.9
2040	27.4	18.9	11.9	11.9
2050	28.6	18.8	11.3	11.9
75–year average: 1976 to 2050	18.9	15.0	11.0	10.9

Note: The Carter proposal is evaluated relative to the wage base in current law to facilitate comparisons with the Hsiao proposal which assumes an insignificantly higher base. Carter, of course, recommends a much larger wage base. The table assumes that both proposals are implemented at the same time.
Source: Congressional Budget Office, *Financing Social Security: Issues for the Short and Long Term*, 1977, p. 50.

of the social security system. Why do we need a compulsory social security plan in a basically free market economy that offers a great variety of private pension plans and would offer even more in the absence of social security? One reason is that our society has shown in many ways that it is not willing to accept the distribution of income resulting from an unfettered free market. In particular, the federal government has shown that it does not wish to see the elderly live in abject poverty and has aided the low-income elderly, earlier with Old Age Assistance and now with the more completely federalized Supplemental Security Income program. Once society decides that it will provide the elderly with basic income support, it of course runs the risk of encouraging irresponsible behavior on the part of those who feel that they will be taken care of in their old age even if they do not put aside financial resources themselves. Thus, social security can be seen as a useful and equitable complement to our welfare system. Put bluntly, it protects society against freeloaders, although this is certainly not the sole historical reason for its existence.

But the fundamental questions is how generous the system has to be. Although it is unlikely that any system will remain constant for seventy-five years, projections of the Carter and Hsiao systems to the middle of the twenty-first century bring their answers to this question into stark contrast. The Carter system appears extraordinarily generous by today's standards. A person earning the median wage through his or her working life would receive $16,382 in benefits per year in today's purchasing power if single, and $24,573 if married. This represents 44 and 66 percent, respectively, of the median wage of $37,232 in 1976 dollars that is projected for the year 2050, assuming real wage growth of 2 percent per year. Couples earning the maximum wage base throughout their lives would receive over $30,000 per year in present day purchasing power!

In contrast, the Hsiao proposal would give benefits in the year 2050 of $8,563 to the median retiree if single, and $12,844 if married. This is only slightly more than half the amount provided by Carter. Is it enough? It would certainly appear to be. Hsiao's tax-free benefit for the median worker in 2050 is approximately equal to the 1975 (taxable) median wage. However, notions of poverty are relative. Our poverty line represents a luxurious income in the less developed world. Similarly, today's median wage may seem like extreme poverty in a future world where the median wage is $37,232.

Nevertheless, it seems highly doubtful that the rapid growth in benefits implied by the Carter option should be built into the law. As noted earlier, it is very much more difficult to make existing law less generous than it is to make it more generous. By keeping costs down, the Hsiao approach provides much more flexibility to adjust benefits upward if they are judged to be too low relative to the standard of living and/or if unexpected changes in demographic and economic variables make benefit increases less costly than they appear to be at the present time. In contrast, if the Carter proposal turns out to be even more costly than expected, it will be very painful to cut back.

Options that reduce the cost of the total system also make it easier to improve the equity of the benefit structure. Any improvement in equity involves relative winners and relative losers. Reform is much easier if the relative losers do not also have to be absolute losers.

More fundamentally, the spread of private pensions, their regulation by the federal government, and their diminished risk because of the Pension Guarantee Corporation all suggest that the argument for a very large social security system that is a good substitute for private pensions is no longer as powerful as it once was. If, despite this increased government intervention or perhaps because of it, private pension systems do not evolve satisfactorily, social security benefits could be raised periodically under the Hsiao option. The Carter option prejudges the issue and automatically builds sufficient growth into social security that it will continue in large part to be a substitute for private pension plans.

It should also be noted that the Carter proposal results in a rapidly growing discrepancy in benefits between those who are newly retired and those who retired a number of years earlier. For example, if the Carter proposal had been adopted in 1976, a person born in 1911 and retiring in 1976, who had median earnings throughout his or her career, would receive a benefit amount of $347. This amount would then be held constant in 1976 dollars. A younger person born in 1916 and retiring in 1981 having earned the median wage would receive $414 in benefits measured in 1976 dollars. Under the Hsiao proposal the latter would receive $366. In other words, under the Hsiao proposal the discrepancy between the standards of living of the newly retired and those who have been retired longer grows much more slowly than under the Carter proposal. Given that the Hsiao proposal costs so much less, it might from time to time allow Congress to increase the real benefits of those already retired as well as the potential benefits of the working population. Such benefit increases would allow the already retired population to share in some of the benefits of the economic growth of the nation—something that would be very difficult to achieve under the much more expensive Carter proposal.

There are, of course, all sorts of different combinations of the Carter and Hsiao proposals that might be considered. To understand these, some knowledge of the mechanics of indexing is required. Because indexing involves inordinately complicated arithmetic, a discussion of complex combinations is confined to the appendix.

Although Carter's short-run financing proposals successfully avoided payroll tax rate increases, his indexing proposal is so expensive that he felt obliged to recommend a tax rate increase for the period 1985 to 2011. He achieves this increase by accelerating a portion of the 2-percentage-point increase scheduled in current law for 2011. A 0.5-percentage-point increase would go into effect in 1985, and a 1.5-percentage-point increase would take effect in 1990.

This acceleration might be prudent even if the Hsiao approach were adopted. It would probably successfully fund the Hsiao option for the next seventy-five years all by itself, but it would be desirable to also adopt Carter's cost-saving dependency test and his increase in the tax rate on the self-employed. As noted earlier, his proposed shift of HI tax increase to the OASDI fund is somewhat dubious, but it would help to mitigate the short-run problem. Unless we have very bad luck, the above proposals would easily finance the Hsiao option over the next seventy-five years. General revenue financing, disproportionate employer tax rate increases, and employer base increases could all be avoided.

There would still be a high probability that the trust funds would have a negative balance in the 1980s, but this is not a serious problem as long as a system is in place that eventually provides surpluses. The burden of social security eases temporarily about the turn of the century when those born during the baby trough of the Great Depression retire. At that time, any trust fund debt can be paid off and surpluses accumulated for the future.

Of course, some would strongly object to the notion of the trust funds going into debt, even temporarily. Once we get used to the notion of a negative trust fund, the discipline imposed by the trust fund concept might erode and lead to unwarranted increases in benefits. If this is considered to be a severe danger, a portion of the tax rate increase could be accelerated further. Something less than the Ford increase of 1.1 percentage points over the period 1978 to 1980 would take care of both the short- and long-run problems under the Hsiao proposal.

Social Security and Capital Formation

Martin Feldstein has argued that the existence of the social security retirement system has had a major negative impact on capital formation in this country. He points out that social security is like a private pension system in that a stream of future benefits is guaranteed the worker, but very much unlike private pension schemes in that the promised stream of benefits will be financed by taxing future workers and is not in the main financed from the return to a portfolio of investments accumulated over an individual's working lifetime. There is a small and declining social security trust fund, but as noted earlier, it only covers a tiny fraction of the total liabilities of the system. Thus the system provides a promise of retirement income without requiring that society accumulate savings to finance it. Payroll taxes with which the worker "buys" the right to future social security benefits are channeled directly to the currently retired population instead of to an earmarked investment portfolio as they would be in most private pension plans.

Although the main effect of social security is to reduce private savings for retirement without putting public savings in their place, it does have an indirect impact that works in the opposite direction. Since a large portion of social security benefits are lost by those who work after age 65, the existence of the system undoubtedly encourages many to retire earlier than they otherwise would. They may decide to save a bit more during their working lifetime to complement their expected social security income.

However, Feldstein believes that this indirect positive impact on savings is overwhelmed by the negative impact of social security's substituting for fully-funded private plans. He estimates that the existence of social security may have reduced our current capital stock by more than $1 trillion or by more than 25 percent.[7] Needless to say, such estimates must be put forward with great uncertainty and many have disputed Feldstein's estimates.[8] However, even if the true impact is a small fraction of Feldstein's estimate, we must reckon with the possibility that social security has had a significant negative impact on economic growth.

This argues for limiting the expansion of the system and is, therefore, another reason for favoring the Hsiao proposal for indexing over President Carter's proposal. It could also be an argument for moving the system in the direction of full funding, that is, for raising payroll taxes to accumulate a larger trust fund. Feldstein believes that we should at least accumulate reserves in this century that could be depleted when the ratio of the retired to working population rises rapidly in the next century. This way, more of the future burden could be borne now by those who will benefit rather than waiting and imposing the entire burden of demographic changes on future generations of workers.

Structural Problems in Social Security

Spouse's Benefit. Individuals retiring at age 65 with a dependent spouse 65 or over receive 150 percent of the single retiree's benefit.

---

[7] Martin Feldstein, "Social Security and Savings," *American Economic Review*, vol. 66 (May 1976), pp. 77–86.

[8] For a discussion, see Alicia Munnell, *The Future of Social Security* (Washington, D.C.: Brookings Institution, 1977), chapter 6. In a yet unpublished paper, Robert Barro argues that social security has no impact on saving at all ("Social Security and Private Saving: Evidence from the U.S.," mimeo., University of Rochester, Rochester, N.Y.).

Spouses can claim benefits based on their individual contributions, but this is clearly not worthwhile when the smaller benefit is less than half the larger benefit.

Two sorts of inequities result from this situation. First, a couple in which one partner earned all the income receives a greater benefit upon retirement than if the same income was earned by both spouses. For example, a middle-income couple retiring in 1976 with a total AME of $439 received an initial monthly benefit of $445 if one spouse earned all the AME, but only $388 if half the income was earned by each spouse. Second, the secondary earner in the family receives no benefits from all his or her contributions unless the value of the benefits is equal to more than 50 percent of those of the primary earner. Even if the secondary worker's benefits are 70 percent of those of the primary worker, the net benefit gain to the couple in return for all the secondary contributions is only about 13 percent $\left(\dfrac{1.7}{1.5}\right)$.

These inequities were clearly less serious when the typical couple only contained one working member, but now that both husbands and wives work outside the home in more than half of all marriages, the implied inequities have become much more serious. The Hsiao panel confronts this problem by recommending that the total AME of a couple be averaged between spouses, with the couple to receive double the PIA that results. In all cases where only one spouse worked, the total benefit would be less than that which results from the current spouse's benefit. However, the progressive nature of the benefit formula ensures that the benefit of a retired couple who divide their AME between them would be higher than that of a single worker who earns the same total AME.

Given that the Hsiao proposal would reduce the costs of the system, the panel recommends that the savings might be used to make the new indexed benefit formula more generous.

Minimum Benefit. The current benefit structure provides a minimum benefit to anyone who qualifies for coverage. In early 1976 that minimum was $101.40 per month. Prior to 1972, the minimum benefit could be justified by the desire to set a floor under the retiree's income because the extant Old Age Assistance (OAA) program provided greatly varying benefits in different parts of the country. However, in 1972, OAA was federalized and the new Supplementary Security Income program (SSI) was created. In early 1976, SSI guaranteed a monthly income of at least $157.70 to a single retiree and $236.60 to a couple. These benefits are indexed to the CPI.

With SSI, the minimum social security benefit is no longer relevant to the really poor retired person. The advantages conferred by the minimum benefit are primarily enjoyed by individuals who worked in covered occupations just long enough to fully qualify for social security, but who worked the rest of their life in an uncovered occupation such as the federal civil service. As a result, many of the beneficiaries of the minimum benefit also enjoy the benefits of some other retirement system and may be quite well off.

Clearly, SSI has now taken care of the original objective of the minimum benefit and there is no reason for its continued existence. The Hsiao panel recommends its elimination.

Retirement Test. An individual under 72 must retire to qualify for social security benefits. Anyone earning less than $2,760 in early 1976 was defined as "retired" and this base is indexed to the CPI. Individuals who continue to work lose $0.50 for every dollar in earnings above the base. Since they must pay payroll taxes on their earnings and perhaps some income tax, the incentive to retire is very high. There is, however, one element of the social security law that serves to offset these disincentives. Benefits increase 1 percent for every extra month worked between ags 62 and 65, and 0.08 percent per month for work beyond age 65. However, this minor work incentive is undoubtedly overwhelmed by the disincentive imposed by the immediate benefit losses imposed by the retirement test.

The retirement test is highly unpopular among beneficiaries, but it is difficult to document its impact. If it were eliminated at age 65 and benefits were paid regardless of whether the beneficiary had retired, there would undoubtedly be some increase in labor force participation. It is often argued that the income tax receipts generated by this increase would pay a part of the cost of eliminating the retirement test. On the other hand, it should be noted that the elimination of the retirement test would provide a lump sum windfall payment to those who now receive no benefit because they chose to work despite the test. Economic theory suggests that such recipients would chose to work fewer hours because of the windfall, but many may not have this choice.

Regardless of the net impact of the test on total work effort, it is safe to conclude that its elimination would increase economic efficiency. Whether or not this reform is a high priority item given the financial stringency faced by the social security system is quite another question. The Hsiao panel took the easy and perhaps the wise way out and suggested that the matter deserves further study before any changes are made.

Appendix: The Arithmetic of Indexing

The Hsiao option is usually referred to as a price-indexing approach while the Carter option is usually called a wage-indexing approach.

If the Hsiao option had been put in place in late 1976 or in early 1977, the panel recommended the following schedule of benefits for retirement at age 65:

Average indexed monthly earnings (AIME)	Initial monthly benefit (PIA)
Less than $200	80% of AIME
$200 to $600	$90 plus 35% of AIME
Over $600	$150 plus 25% of AIME

The beneficiary's AIME is computed by converting earnings since 1950 into 1976 dollars, summing the individual years and averaging over the number of months since 1950, with the worst five years of earnings omitted. This solves the problem posed by the current non-indexed calculation of the AME which discriminates against those who earned more of their income early in life when the dollar was worth more.

Each year the formula is adjusted by raising the dollar amounts in the formula $200, $600, $90, and $150 by the rate of inflation. The percentage terms (80%, 35%, 25%) would be held constant. For example, the rate of price increase between early 1976 and early 1977 was 5.9 percent. Those retiring in late 1977 or early 1978 would have their AIMEs calculated in 1977 dollars and the schedule would be:

AIME	PIA
Less than $212	80% of AIME
$212 to $635	$95 plus 35% of AIME
Over $635	$159 plus 25% of AIME

This approach ensures that the ratio of the PIA to lifetime *real* earnings is not affected by inflation. Note that the current double-indexing approach makes the mistake of indexing the percentage terms in the benefit formula rather than the dollar amounts; the ratio of benefits to earnings is therefore very directly affected by inflation.

In the Carter approach, the dollar amounts are indexed by the rate of increase of the average money wage rather than by the rate of increase in prices. If the economy is growing, wages increase more rapidly than prices. Therefore, the size of the brackets would typically increase more rapidly under the Carter option than under the Hsiao option. The Carter AIME is calculate by converting past earnings into present-day wage equivalents. Put another way, wages earned in year x are inflated by the percentage wage increase since year x rather than by the price increase as under Hsiao. Because this would result in a higher AIME under Carter than under the Hsiao definition, the dollar size of the benefit brackets would have to be larger initially to make total costs initially equal to Hsiao's. The Hsiao formula was, in turn, chosen to provide a system in which the initial cost and benefit distribution approximated that resulting from current law.

It is crucially important to note that the future generosity of the social security system is determined largely by the way in which the dollar amounts (the brackets in the benefit formula) are indexed. This is what determines the future ratio of benefits to earnings. The method chosen for computing the AIME is very much less important. For example, if the Carter approach to computing the AIME were combined with the Hsiao approach for computing the brackets, one would have to begin with wider brackets but the long-run costs would be similar to those implied by the pure Hsiao option. Similarly, the Hsiao approach for calculating the AIME combined with the Carter approach for indexing brackets would have costs similar to those of the pure Carter option.

A result between Carter and Hsiao could be obtained by price-indexing plus some portion of the real wage gain. A similar result could be obtained by indexing to the change in the CPI plus 1 percent. This would be dangerous, however, because there is no guarantee that real wages will rise on average more than 1 percent per year in the future just because they have in the past.

Clearly, there is an infinity of options that combine the two approaches. However, it is important to repeat one of the major arguments made in chapter 7. If the Hsiao approach is chosen, it becomes more likely that an occasional discretionary increase will be possible, which has the practical impact of achieving a result between Hsiao and Carter for future retirees while allowing the current retired population some share of the benefits of real growth.

8

NATIONAL DEFENSE

There is no part of the budget so important as national defense. Our very survival as a nation may ultimately depend on making the correct decisions in this area. And yet, there is no finite expenditure of resources that can guarantee complete invulnerability to foreign attack. The relevant choices have to be made under conditions of great uncertainty. We must ask, first, what are the risks attached to various foreign policy stances? Second, how can those risks be reduced by various types of defense spending? Third, how much do we want to reduce those risks by drawing economic resources away from private sector and other domestic government activities?

Since an analysis of the objectives of our foreign policy is beyond the scope of this discussion, this chapter takes our current foreign policy stances as given. Past trends in defense spending are discussed, and some of the major spending issues now before the president and Congress are analyzed.

Past Decline in the Defense Burden

Table 17 shows defense outlays both in current and constant dollars since 1956. Current outlays as a percentage of GNP, also shown, is an imperfect but useful indicator of the economic burden that our defense budget imposes on society. In 1956, 9.7 percent of GNP was

This chapter was written with the assistance of Lawrence J. Korb. It summarizes many of the major issues considered in Korb's *The Price of Preparedness: The FY 1978–1982 Defense Program* (Washington, D.C.: American Enterprise Institute, 1977).

Table 17

DEFENSE OUTLAYS IN CURRENT AND IN 1972 DOLLARS AND RELATIVE TO GNP, 1956–1976

(in billions of dollars)

Year	Current Dollar Outlays	Outlays as % of GNP	Outlays in 1972 Dollars
1956	39.8	9.7	73.0
1961	46.6	9.2	74.8
1966	55.9	7.8	77.7
1967	69.1	8.9	93.2
1968	79.4	9.6	102.2
1969	80.2	8.9	98.8
1970	79.3	8.3	91.1
1971	76.8	7.5	82.3
1972	77.4	7.0	77.4
1973	75.1	6.1	70.5
1974	78.6	5.8	68.3
1975	86.6	6.0	67.0
1976	90.0	5.6	64.6

Source: *The Budget of the United States Government, Fiscal Year 1978*, table 22, p. 436.

devoted to defense, but by 1966 that proportion had fallen to 7.8 percent. The Vietnam War temporarily raised the percentage to 9.6 percent in 1968, but, with the exception of a slight rise during the recession of 1975, the ratio has fallen steadily since that time to 5.6 percent in 1976.

The fall in the share of GNP devoted to defense actually understates the decline in the true economic burden imposed by our defense effort. The budget, of course, only reflects expenditures of money. Prior to the All Volunteer Force instituted in 1973, individuals were drafted into military service at rates of pay below those in private life for comparable employment. Therefore, in addition to all the other sacrifices involved in military service, many made a substantial monetary sacrifice which was not reflected in the federal budget. With the advent of the All Volunteer Force, the budget has become a much better indicator of the real monetary value of our defense effort. In addition, about 8 percent of the present budget funds the cost of retirement benefits for those who served in previous years. Had a trust fund been in existence over the past three decades, the decline in the real value of the budget would be even greater.

While the economic burden imposed by the defense effort is

roughly measured by the share of money GNP devoted to defense, what we get for this sacrifice is very crudely measured by the real value of defense spending. In 1972 dollars, $64.6 billion was spent in 1976, an amount significantly lower than the $73.0 billion spent in 1956. However, such measures can be misleading. A given real-dollar input level can be used with various degrees of efficiency, and it is conceivable that the quality of the output obtained with fewer dollars in 1976 was higher than that obtained in 1956.[1] The degree of protection obtained with a given real input of resources also depends crucially on the defense effort undertaken by our potential adversaries.

Some Conceptual Difficulties

Although the analysis of social programs is often highly complex and always difficult, the problems seem simple compared with those facing a defense analyst. A multitude of highly uncertain variables must be considered in each important decision, and the decisions made today may not have much influence on our defense posture for many years to come. For example, a new ship funded in the 1978 budget will not be ready for action until the mid-1980s and then might remain operational for another twenty years. The B-1 bomber has been debated and developed over a fifteen-year period. While the development of a weapons system proceeds, technological change is occurring at a rapid rate and often requires extensive modifications and delays.

Moreover, every change in our defense strategy is likely to promote countermoves on the part of potential adversaries which may alter predictions regarding the nature of future conflicts. There are, in turn, a multitude of options available for contending with any specific contingency.

The 1978 Budget and Long-Run Projections of Defense Spending

Given the uncertainty surrounding defense strategy, a rather remarkable consensus concerning the defense budget has developed since 1975. There is now a widespread belief that the decline in the real value of defense spending must be halted. The debates focus on whether the spending increases should be somewhat greater than the

---

[1] The introduction of PPBS and systems analysis into the Pentagon in the early 1960s undoubtedly increased the efficiency with which each dollar is used. Whether the improvement has offset the decline in real expeditures is, however, much more difficult to determine.

expected growth of GNP over the next five years or whether the budget should do little more than provide for price inflation, thus growing slightly less than GNP. It is within these rather narrow limits that the bulk of the argument occurs. That is not to say that the debate lacks intensity. This year, controversy over the size of the defense budget made it extremely difficult for the House of Representatives to pass its first budget resolution. But major differences of opinion involve fairly small percentage differences in the total size of the defense budget, and the degree of hostility against defense spending has most certainly diminished greatly since the worst of the reaction toward the Vietnam War.

In discussing defense budgets, the longtime lag between planning for an expenditure and actually making it requires that total obligational authority (TOA) should be emphasized rather than outlays. Table 18 shows defense TOA and outlays in the Ford, Carter, and congressional versions of the 1978 budget. The initial Carter reductions from the Ford budget (which do not bear much relationship to the $5 or $7 billion cuts discussed during the presidential campaign) primarily involve either stretching out procurement or postponing certain spending decisions. Once these decisions are made, they will of course have significant longer run implications, but at the present time it appears that Carter's spending recommendations for the long run will differ very little from those that would have occurred if Ford had remained in office.

In the First Budget Resolution, Congress passed a target spend-

Table 18

FORD, CARTER, AND CONGRESSIONAL DEFENSE BUDGETS, 1978
(in billions of dollars)

	TOA	Outlays
Ford	$122.8	$112.3
Carter[a]	120.1	111.9
Congress (First Budget Resolution)	118.5	111.0

[a] The amounts shown are from the February budget revisions. By the *Mid-Session Review of the 1978 Budget*, Carter's amounts had changed to $122.3 (TOA) and $113.0 outlays. However, the differences do not reflect policy changes. They primarily reflect changed estimates, owing partly to spending delays in 1977 that will be made up in 1978.

Source: Office of Management and Budget, *Fiscal Year 1978 Budget Revisions* (February 1977), pp. 27–28.

ing level for the national defense category that was lower than in the Carter budget. This target is not meant to determine a specific defense program—the armed services and the relevant appropriation committees are supposed to do that within the limits set by the First Congressional Budget Resolution. Without a specific program one cannot make long-run projections of the implications of the congressional spending targets. I therefore provide the Ford projections as a basis for a discussion of the options facing the armed services and appropriations committees (table 19).

The projections should not be taken as predictions. They represent the long-run implications of the 1978 defense budget as it was proposed by Ford in January 1977. Even if he had been reelected, these projections would have been altered from time to time because of changes in policy that he may have recommended as conditions changed and as Congress accepted some of his proposals and rejected others. Moreover, the projections are based on assumptions regarding future inflation, future pay raises, and future costs of complex weapons systems that must, by their very nature, remain highly tenuous.

Table 19

FORD PROJECTIONS OF NATIONAL DEFENSE, BUDGET AUTHORITY AND OUTLAYS, FISCAL 1978–1982
(in billions of dollars)

Item	1978	1979	1980	1981	1982
Budget Authority					
Military personnel	$ 27.7	$ 29.1	$ 30.5	$ 31.9	$ 33.5
Retired military	9.1	9.7	10.5	11.2	11.8
Operations &					
maintenance	34.9	36.6	38.3	40.6	42.3
Procurement	35.1	39.8	46.1	51.3	55.3
Research,					
development, test,					
& evaluation	12.0	13.0	14.5	15.1	16.8
Military construction	1.4	4.5	3.2	3.6	3.6
Other	2.6	2.7	2.8	3.0	3.5
Total Outlays	$123.2	$135.4	$145.8	$156.7	$166.7
Current dollars	$110.1	$121.2	$133.7	$145.5	$156.3
% of GNP	5.4	5.3	5.3	5.3	5.4
FY 1978 dollars	$110.1	$115.2	$120.9	$125.6	$129.0
% of real GNP	5.4	5.4	5.3	5.3	5.2

Source: Lawrence J. Korb, *The Price of Preparedness: The FY 1978–1982 Defense Program* (Washington, D.C.: American Enterprise Institute, 1977).

Indeed, it is quite possible that unexpected changes in such assumptions may be more important to future defense costs than the program changes from the Ford budget advocated by Carter and the Congress.

The projections show current dollar outlays rising about as rapidly as GNP through 1982. The real value of defense outlays rises slightly less than real GNP, which implies that the prices of defense goods and services are expected to rise somewhat more rapidly than the general price level. It should be noted that part of this relative price rise is illusory. Because productivity increases in our defense establishment are impossible to measure, they are considered to be zero for statistical purposes. Since some productivity increases are likely, the rise in the prices of defense goods and services tend to be somewhat overstated and we are likely to get slightly more for our money than is indicated by the projections of real spending.

The projections under *Budget Authority* indicate that the military personnel, operations and maintenance, and procurement categories will absorb about 80 percent of the entire defense budget over the 1978–1982 period. There are major concerns regarding the future costs of military personnel, although the Ford budget projects that such costs will decline relatively from 22.5 percent of total budget authority in fiscal 1978 to 20.0 percent in fiscal 1982. The salary increases implicit in these projections average slightly less than 6 percent per year while manpower levels are expected to remain constant at about 2.1 million. Some experts ask whether such salary increases will attract a sufficient supply of volunteers over a time period when employment opportunities in the private sector are likely to improve rapidly and the supply of potential recruits will be declining because of the decline in birth rates in the 1960s.

If the quantity and/or quality of recruits begins to decline, the debate over the desirability of the volunteer army is sure to gain in intensity. Some will advocate a return to conscription to dampen the rise in defense budget costs. However, budget costs should not be a prime consideration in this debate. While conscription may lower money costs slightly in the near term, it will definitely raise the social and economic costs of the defense effort as personnel are conscripted who could be more productive in the private sector. Moreover, in the long run conscription may not even save money, as the increased training costs brought about by high turnover outweigh savings in compensation.

It may, of course, be possible to use current money outlays on personnel more effectively to attract personnel and to encourage reenlistment. For example, the Congressional Budget Office notes that while the retirement system provides significant rewards for staying in the services over twenty years, it does not do much to encourage reenlistment for shorter periods. The CBO also suggests a reexamination of certain in-kind, nontaxed benefits such as housing and subsistence allowances and asks whether taxed money payments might be more effective at recruiting and retaining personnel.[2] Of course, the same potential trade-off between nontaxed fringe benefits and taxed salary income also exists in the private sector, but the nature of the trade-off is by no means clear. CBO also believs that savings are possible by reducing training periods. However, some evidence exists that there is a relationship between the length of training and discipline, and the savings may not be worth the eventual cost in terms of lowered personnel effectiveness.[3] Increasing the number of women in the armed forces or altering the physical standards for male recruits is an alternative way to provide a larger pool of potential recruits at a given compensation level.

While there is a widespread agreement that the decline in the real value of defense spending should be reversed, it is important to note that this change in the national mood has crucial implications for the nation's overall budget strategy. Since the late 1960s the decline in the relative importance of defense spending has been used to accommodate the financial needs of programs such as social security, Medicaid, and Medicare, which have built-in growth rates that tend to exceed the growth in GNP. In other words, increases in the relative burden imposed by social programs have been counterbalanced by relative declines in the defense burden. If the defense burden now becomes relatively constant, there will be a very strong tendency for the total federal budget to grow more rapidly than GNP unless the few controllable nondefense programs are squeezed severely or there are structural changes imposed on domestic entitlement programs.

Proposed changes of this type will, of course, generate conflict, and because defense outlays are more "controllable" than most, there will be strong pressure to keep their growth below those in the Ford projections. There will also be charges that there is much "waste" or "fat" in the defense budget. These charges will have some merit since it is never hard to find waste in any bureaucracy, let alone one as large as the Pentagon. However, in assessing such charges, it is im-

[2] Congressional Budget Office, *Budget Options for Fiscal Year 1978*, February 1977, pp. 59–67.

[3] U.S. Congress, House Armed Services Committee, *Report of the Special Sub-Committee on Disciplinary Problems in the U.S. Navy*, January 2, 1973, p. 17671.

portant to remember that there is no major part of the budget that has been squeezed as hard or has received scrutiny as intense as that applied to the defense budget since the Vietnam War. While there is undoubtedly some waste remaining, it may now be more productive to turn over search for waste toward the social programs.

Issues in Defense Procurement

The remainder of this chapter focuses on certain controversial procurement issues that are likely to be at the heart of any budget debate over defense over the next few years. Table 19 implies that procurement absorbed 28.5 percent of TOA in Ford's 1978 budget and this category was expected to grow to 33.2 percent of TOA by 1982. Within the procurement category, the most difficult decisions involve purchase of the aircraft and ships required to modernize our forces. Table 20 outlines the Ford plans in these areas. The proposed authorizations for aircraft procurement, shipbuilding, and ship conversion are $19.8 billion in 1978, growing to $32.1 billion in 1982. These items will absorb well over half the total procurement budget over the 1978–1982 period.

Table 20

AIRCRAFT AND SHIPBUILDING COSTS, FY 1978–1982
(in billions of dollars)

Item	1978	1979	1980	1981	1982	Total 1978–82
Aircraft Procurement						
Air Force	8.7	9.2	11.3	11.7	12.6	53.5
Navy	3.7	4.3	4.6	4.9	4.5	22.0
Army	0.7	1.1	1.2	1.4	1.5	5.9
Marines	0.2	0.2	0.2	0.3	0.4	1.3
Total	13.3	14.8	17.3	18.3	19.0	82.7
Minus B-1	1.7	2.6	2.8	3.0	2.8	12.9
Tactical air forces	11.6	12.2	14.5	15.3	16.2	69.8
Shipbuilding and conversion	6.5	8.2	9.9	10.7	13.1	48.4
Minus Trident	1.8	1.1	1.9	1.2	2.0	8.0
General purpose ships	4.7	7.1	8.0	9.5	11.1	40.4

Source: Lawrence J. Korb, *The Price of Preparedness: The FY 1978–1982 Defense Program*, table 9 (Washington, D.C.: American Enterprise Institute, 1977), p. 14.

Aircraft Procurement. In a recent study of defense policy, Barry Blechman and his coauthors noted: "More than to any other type of combat force, the United States has applied its ingenuity, technological prowess, and productive capacity to the development of aircraft, their electronic subsystems, and their ordnance. Consequently, U.S. aircraft are unrivaled in performance and reliability."[4] But they also emphasize that the growing sophistication of aircraft has been accompanied by a rapid rise in their per unit cost, and since an aircraft can only be in one place at one time, budget restraints force a trade-off between quality and quantity in aircraft procurement.

It is also necessary to decide what proportion of aircraft procurement should be devoted to close-in support of ground troops, what proportion should be devoted to control of the air, and what proportion should be devoted to developing the capability for deep strikes into the territory of potential adversaries. In deciding on the appropriate allocation between missions it is necessary to note that more heavily armed forces may in some circumstances be a substitute for strengthening air cover and that unmanned aircraft and missiles may be a substitute for manned aircraft for the purposes of making strikes into enemy territory.

For fiscal 1978, Ford recommended budget authority for the purchase of over seven hundred aircraft to be used for ground support, maintenance of air superiority, and deep-strike missions. A very large share of Ford's proposed aircraft procurement program involves the purchase of tactical aircraft that are primarily designed for air combat, but which can have secondary roles in ground support and interdiction. Included are:

(1) *The high performance F-14A, with a unit cost of $25.4 million.* The total cost of the program, including past and future authorizations, will be $12.8 billion of which $1.8 billion was requested in FY 1978.

(2) *The F-15, with a unit cost of $16.8 million.* The total cost of the program is $12.6 billion of which $0.9 billion was requested in 1978.

(3) *The F-18, which will come in both aerial combat and ground support versions.* The unit cost is $16.0 million.

---

[4] Barry B. Blechman et al., "Toward a New Consensus in U.S. Defense Policy," in *Setting National Priorities: The Next Ten Years,* ed. Henry Owen and Charles L. Schultze (Washington, D.C., Brookings Institution, 1976), p. 101.

The total cost is $12.8 billion, of which $0.8 billion was requested in 1978. President Ford also recommended the procurement of the A-10 and advanced attack helicopters (AAH), primarily for ground support missions. The A-10 has a unit cost of $6.1 million while the AAH costs $700,000. President Ford asked for $1.1 billion in budget authority for these two programs in 1978.

He also recommended proceeding with the B-1 bomber at a total long-run cost of over $22 billion. In his February budget revisions, Carter recommended a slowdown in the rate of production of the F-15 and B-1 until requirements could be studied more carefully, but accepted the other Ford recommendations.

Probably the most intense debate has involved the development of the B-1 bomber. On June 30, 1977, Carter announced that he was halting production entirely, but would continue research and development. The B-1 is a formidable weapon which can strike deep into enemy territory at high speeds while flying low enough to evade enemy air defenses. It is also an extremely expensive weapon costing over $100 million per plane. In addition, it will require additional investments in aerial tankers and base facilities.

Two questions must be asked in assessing President Carter's decision. First, is it necessary to supplement our land- and submarine-based missiles with bombers to ensure that we have retaliatory capacity against the Soviet Union? Second, if it is necessary to complement our missile system, is the B-1 a cost-effective complement? In answer to the first question, it does appear that a complementary force is necessary. Currently, the United States has only half the destructive capacity of the Soviet Union if the bomber fleet is not counted. The United States has an advantage in the number of warheads and in their accuracy, but given the nature of the limits imposed by the current SALT provisions, the Soviets will be able to improve both the number and accuracy of their warheads while American power will be held constant.

While prudence seems to require the maintenance of some sort of bomber fleet, it is more difficult to know whether the B-1 is the most cost-effective alternative. Alternatives include modernizing a portion of our B-52s, stretched F-111 Bs, or modified 747s that could stand-off from the Soviet borders and serve as airborne platforms for launching the cruise missile. Carter has opted for modernizing later models of the B-52 and equipping them with cruise missiles. However, the president noted that his decision might be reversed if warranted by changing conditions. Much depends on the outcome of the current SALT talks. Limits on the cruise missile, or, at the other extreme, a total breakdown of the talks could induce Carter to produce the B-1 bomber despite its high cost.

Shipbuilding. The modernization of the Navy is an extremely expensive endeavor which in Ford's program absorbs over one-fifth the total procurement budget for the next five years. There is a widespread consensus that modernization is required, but there is also considerable confusion about the forms it should take.

Between 1968 and 1976, the number of ships in our surface combatant fleet fell by 50 percent from 350 to 175. This occurred because a large number of ships of World War II vintage had to be retired almost simultaneously owing to their bloc obsolescence. They were not replaced as the competing financial demands of the Vietnam War caused new shipbuilding to decline precipitously. (Only 8 new ships were constructed annually in the 1967–1972 period compared with 45 in the period 1962–1967.)

While the size of the American surface fleet has been declining, the Soviet Union's has increased in size. Overall, the Soviet Navy remains somewhat inferior to the American fleet, but the demands on it are much less. Moreover, it now has the capability to venture out of Soviet coastal waters and to make its presence felt in the Mediterranean, the Indian Ocean, the South Atlantic, and the Caribbean.

Although the Ford administration strongly supported a major shipbuilding effort, it vacillated about the size of that effort and about the appropriate mission for the modernized navy. Currently, the United States Navy has two principal missions. It has the defensive mission of protecting sea lanes to ensure that this nation can use them for obtaining raw materials and resupplying and reinforcing our overseas allies. It also has an offensive mission in that it maintains some capability to launch attacks against the well-defended homeland of our principal adversary. The question is which mission should be emphasized by the shipbuilding program, or should the program attempt to maintain the current balance between the two missions? The defensive mission primarily requires an antisubmarine force consisting of smaller ships such as frigates, fast missile boats, and medium-size destroyers and cruisers. The aggressive mission requires large Nimitz-class carriers and attack cruisers, along with numerous escort vessels equipped with sophisticated air defense systems—an extremely expensive proposition. Whether the cost is worth it depends partially on whether air defense systems would be capable of protecting huge carriers and other large vessels in the event of a major war.

The Ford budget seemed to shift the balance somewhat in favor of the defensive, "sea-control" mission. After much dispute within the administration, the 1978 budget advocated the construction of 157 ships in the 1978–1982 period at a cost of $48 billion. Although Ford had earlier approved a House Armed Services Committee decision to proceed with a Nimitz-class super-carrier, the 1978 budget requested a recision of the relevant appropriations. Ford did not, however, ignore the Navy's attack role and recommended two medium-sized, conventionally powered carriers, two attack nuclear cruisers, and ten large escort vessels equipped with sophisticated air defenses.

The Carter budget revisions tilted the balance somewhat more toward the sea control mission. He supported the Ford decision to cancel the Nimitz-class carrier and is apparently canceling the two attack cruisers. However, his budget retains the ten escort vessels— raising a question about what they will be defending.

It is apparent that neither the Ford and Carter administrations nor the Congress has yet carefully thought through the extent to which the Navy shóuld emphasize its attack capability. Until this is done, the Navy's shipbuilding budget will lack a coherent strategy and the Navy will continue to be the only service without an explicitly defined mission.

9

HEALTH

President Carter, like President Ford before him, has to contend with soaring federal health costs. The different reactions to this difficult problem as the 1978 budget was passed from one to the other reveal one of the more interesting differences in the philosophies of the two presidents. The dimensions of the problem are revealed by past trends in federal health expenditures.

Past Budget Trends

The health budget function is divided into four categories: health care services, health research and education, prevention and control of health problems, and health planning and construction. In the late 1950s and early 1960s total spending on all four categories amounted to less than 0.3 percent of GNP. The big change in federal policy occurred in fiscal 1966 when the Medicaid and Medicare programs were initiated. Medicaid is administered by state and local governments, with federal financial assistance provided by a categorical grant. It provides medical services to welfare recipients and, in some states, to the nonwelfare poor. Medicare provides health care to the elderly and is federally administered through the social security system. Primarily as a result of these two programs, total federal health spending jumped from 0.4 percent of GNP in 1965 to 0.9 percent in 1966 and to 1.2 percent in 1967. Since that time, the growth in the ratio has continued, though at a slower rate, reaching 2.1 percent of GNP in 1976. Almost all the growth in the ratio has occurred in the health care services function which contains the Medicaid and Medicare programs. The remaining three functions grew only from 0.2 to 0.3 percent of GNP over the ten-year period.

111

Table 21

FEDERAL HEALTH OUTLAYS, 1966–1976
(in millions of dollars)

	1966	1967	1968	1969	1970	1971
Health Care Services						
Amount	$1,153	$4,909	$7,593	$ 9,537	$10,648	$12,107
% of GNP	0.2	0.6	0.9	1.1	1.1	1.2
Health Research and Education						
Amount	948	1,229	1,405	1,459	1,577	1,687
% of GNP	0.1	0.2	0.2	0.2	0.2	0.2
Prevention and Control of Health Problems						
Amount	275	313	318	348	362	459
% of GNP	a	a	a	a	a	0.1
Health Planning and Construction						
Amount	262	311	393	415	469	465
% of GNP	a	a	0.1	0.1	0.1	a
TOTAL						
Amount	$2,638	$6,759	$9,708	$11,758	$13,051	$14,716
% of GNP	0.4	0.9	1.2	1.3	1.4	1.5

a Less than 0.5 percent.
Source: *The Budget of the United States Government*, various years.

The relative growth in health care expenditures was spurred both by increases in quantity consumed and by the intimately related rise in relative prices. Over the period 1966–1976 the medical care component of the consumer price index about doubled while the overall index rose about 75 percent. Over the same period, total private and public health care expenditures have risen from about 6 to over 8 percent of GNP.

It should be noted that the increase in federal spending on Medicaid and Medicare greatly exaggerates the growth in the burden imposed on the economy by health care costs. While the programs undoubtedly increased the demand for health services by lowering costs to the poor and the elderly and so increased some health spending, a very large portion of federal health spending simply replaced private health spending that would otherwise have drawn on the same economic resources now absorbed by Medicaid and Medicare.

However, both Ford and Carter promised to balance some future

| | 1972 | 1973 | 1974 | 1975 | 1976 | Annual Growth Rate | | |
						1966-71	1971-76	1966-76
	$14,538	$15,476	$18,502	$23,405	$28,655	60.0	18.8	37.9
	1.3	1.3	1.4	1.6	1.8			
	1,952	2,272	2,334	2,677	3,086	12.2	12.8	12.5
	0.2	0.2	0.2	0.2	0.2			
	541	638	750	883	963	10.8	16.0	13.4
	0.1	0.1	0.1	0.1	0.1			
	443	449	494	687	752	12.2	10.1	11.1
	a	a	a	0.1	0.1			
	$17,471	$18,832	$22,074	$27,647	$33,448	41.0	17.8	28.9
	1.6	1.5	1.6	1.9	2.1			

budget without greatly increasing tax burdens. (Ford wanted to balance the 1979 budget; Carter has chosen 1981.) As a result, they focused their initiatives primarily on the government's budget costs rather than on increasing the efficiency of total private and public health spending. The most severe budget problem is posed by the health care services category which since 1971 has grown at an annual rate of over 18 percent (see table 21). In fiscal 1976 alone, the growth rate was over 22 percent! Both presidents reacted to this explosion, but neither really faced up to the economic phenomena underlying the growing health burden.

Controlling the Health Budget

The Ford budget attempted to control costs very differently for Medicaid and Medicare, even though they reflect the same economic phenomena. Medicaid was lumped with nineteen small categorical grant programs into a block grant program, called Financial Assistance for Health Care. In effect, the Ford proposal told the states to solve the Medicaid cost control problem.

A strong argument can be made for consolidating a large portion of the multitude of categorical grant programs in the health area. These grants now subsidize states and localities to provide community health centers, maternal and child health programs, family planning, migrant health programs, programs for hypertension, and other special-need programs. They tend to focus on narrowly defined health problems where the need is likely to vary greatly from region to region. As a result, two major problems emerge. First, it is extremely difficult to administer a program from Washington that focuses on a narrowly defined problem or client group. To ensure that states and localities actually spend the money according to the intent of the law, the relevant federal agency has to construct a complex administrative apparatus which inevitably generates piles of red tape. Second, the high federal subsidy contained in most of these programs induces states and localities to create very specific programs whether or not a serious need exists for them. States and localities have a tendency to view such programs more as a mechanism for attracting federal dollars than as a mechanism for solving a high priority health problem. Consequently, the geographic distribution of funds begins to depend more on the skill of the "grantsmen" at the state and local level than on the distribution of health needs.

The Ford consolidation would instead have distributed health care assistance through a formula based on the number of poor persons in a state, overall state tax effort, and average state per capita income. States would then have the freedom to use the grants for the health needs that they felt were most pressing.

A purist might argue that there is no need for any federal grant at all: if states find health needs that require financial assistance, they should be willing to raise their own taxes to pay for them. If the taxes now financing federal grants were eliminated, states and localities would have a larger tax base from which to draw such revenues. There is much to be said for the purist approach—Governor Reagan argued for it for a brief time during the 1976 primaries—but it is not politically feasible at the present time given that states and localities have become thoroughly addicted to federal support in the health area. Moreover, many would argue that the purist approach is inequitable in that not all states have the same ability to afford health programs. The Ford approach attempted to put states on an equal footing in their ability to finance health care. It would certainly reduce federal and state administrative costs in comparison with the current fragmented system and, if one has confidence in the democratic process at the state and local level, it should improve the equity and efficiency of health programs.

While the consolidation of nineteen minor categorical programs into a single block grant program appears eminently sensible, the Ford proposal was distorted by the inclusion of the Medicaid program, which in dollar cost overwhelms all the others. The decision to include Medicaid was clearly made on budgetary grounds rather than on conceptual grounds, for, as argued below, that program faces fundamental economic problems of national proportions that will not be cured by dumping it on the states.

Although the Ford health block grant program implied 1978 outlays virtually identical to outlays projected for the current categorical programs, including Medicaid, it contemplated major budget savings in the long run because it recommended that the block grant's total value be increased at only 5 percent per year. In the face of a Medicaid bill that rose at almost 19 percent per year between 1971 and 1976 and which in the absence of the block grant was expected by the Ford budget to rise at 15 percent per year between 1977 and 1979, the establishment of the block grant program would require major cutbacks in Medicaid at the state level unless states were willing to finance cost increases out of their own tax revenues. More specifically, even if the growth in Medicaid in the absence of the block grant slowed to 10 percent per year after 1979, the total expenditure in 1982 would exceed $18 billion. The Ford grant would supply only $16 billion. Making states face the choice of cutting Medicaid or raising taxes would clearly be more a move in the direction of the aforementioned purist approach, but just as Reagan's purist proposal met with less than overwhelming approval, the Ford proposal was doomed to failure because Congress is not yet willing to make states bite that kind of bullet.

Given this political reality, it is perhaps a shame that Medicaid was included in the otherwise appealing Ford proposal. However, it should be noted that the Carter pledge to balance the budget in 1981 will require biting a whole arsenal of bullets. It would therefore not be surprising to see the resurrection of some sort of block grant proposal in future Carter budgets. Such a proposal is unlikely to include Medicaid, but the consolidation of other minor programs might be a rational approach to reducing the growth in outlays in the long run, because states and localities should be willing to accept slower outlay growth in return for more freedom in choosing how to spend the money.

Regarding Medicare, Ford made two proposals. The first was a structural reform aimed more at economic efficiency and equity than at budget restraint. Currently, the patient pays a deductible and then pays nothing for the next sixty days in the hospital. After sixty days the patient must pay the whole bill; this clearly can create extreme hardship for those with long-term illnesses. Ford wanted to offer protection against such catastrophies and suggested that the extra cost of catastrophic insurance be financed by having the patient pay 10 percent of hospital bills until his or her cost reached $500. This coinsurance feature of the Ford proposal would save money in two ways. It would directly reduce Medicare reimbursements and would also reduce hospital utilization because doctors who know that patients are sharing in the cost will be less likely to prescribe stays that are of marginal therapeutic value. The Ford plan thus rests on a solid conceptual foundation. It prevents the elderly from being financially devastated by a long-term illness, while at the same time resulting in more efficient hospital utilization and reduced federal outlays.

A similar proposal was made for the Supplemental Medicaid Insurance program (part B of Medicare), which finances doctors' services. The deductible would be indexed for inflation, and the patient would bear 10 percent of costs up to a maximum patient contribution of $250. While these proposals rest on a solid conceptual base, they do not, on balance, save much money. The increased patient cost-sharing was expected to save $2.7 billion by fiscal 1979 but the catastrophic insurance was expected to cost $2.4 billion—net saving of $300 million or less than 1 percent of the expected Medicare bill of 1979. Moreover, it should be noted that any estimate of the cost of catastrophic protection must remain highly tenuous. Although private insurance companies are offering catastrophic plans at low rates, we have not had a great deal of experience with such insurance plans, and it is conceivable that they will encourage longer stays and more expensive treatment than is assumed by the cost estimate cited above. But even if the Ford plan saves no money at all, it does represent a significant conceptual improvement in the Medicare system.

Some opposed the Ford coinsurance plan on grounds that it would impose an unwarranted financial burden on the elderly. In response, it should be emphasized that Medicare is not an income-related program: the elderly benefit whether they are rich or poor. A very large portion of the recipient population could easily afford

116

the coinsurance payment and should be willing to make this sacrifice to avoid the threat of the huge bills that can result from a catastrophic illness. For those who are truly poor, it is possible to design a program that waives the coinsurance payment, although this would introduce a means test into Medicare for the first time.

Ford proposed a saving that was more significant, but less appealing conceptually, by recommending that increases in Medicare payment rates be restricted to 7 percent for per diem hospital fees and 7 percent for physician fees. Even this increase would be disallowed if it raised fees above the level prevailing in each locality in 1977. The ceilings on payment increases were to prevail in 1977 and 1978. Ford also suggested that depreciation payments for hospitals be approved only for new construction that has the approval of state health planning agencies. The total saving would be $3.4 billion by fiscal 1979 or over 10 percent of the expected Medicare bill. The apparent saving is large, but arbitrary ceilings on reimbursements are never easy to administer and may result in a diminution of the quality of care available to Medicare patients.

The Carter budget revisions rejected the Ford block grant proposal and the structural reform of Medicare. It attempted to reduce the Medicaid and Medicare budgets and restrain all health costs by imposing price controls on hospitals. Increases in charges would be generally limited to 9 percent with a 1 percent limit for exceptions. An additional exception can be granted if fee increases greater than 9 percent can be justified by increased nonsupervisory labor costs. A further limit is placed on capital expenditures by hospitals. Such expenditures are limited to $2.5 billion or half the $5 billion expended in 1976. The Carter price controls were expected to reduce Medicare outlays by $695 million in 1978. This compares with the $1.8 billion saved by Ford's more stringent reimbursement controls. The Carter program also saves $134 million in Medicaid outlays.

Any arbitrary system of price controls is a nightmare to administer. The Carter administration hopes to limit the necessary increase in the bureaucracy by relying on local health system agencies and by limiting reimbursements by third-party groups such as Medicaid, Medicare, and private health insurers. Nevertheless, it is safe to predict that the control system will find it extraordinarily difficult to limit costs while maintaining the quality of care and avoiding inefficiencies. For example, the fact that increased labor costs can be passed forward will diminish the degree to which wage demands are resisted and will encourage overhiring.

In summary, Ford's proposals for Medicare cost-sharing and

catastrophe insurance reflect sound economic principles. His transfer of Medicaid to the states is consistent with the philosophy of the "New Federalism," but has more of the appearance of passing the buck. His arbitrary reimbursement controls are not consistent with any readily apparent philosophy or economic principle, but may instead be interpreted as pure pragmatism. In contrast, there is no reliance on economic incentives in the Carter approach. It instead manifests confidence that health costs can be controlled with an appropriate government regulatory apparatus.

But both Ford's reimbursement controls and Carter's price controls attack the symptoms rather than causes of soaring health costs. In the long run they are likely to be as effective as King Canute's injunction against the tides. A major cause of rising costs is our method of financing health expenditures. Over 90 percent of all hospital costs are paid by government or some private insurer. Whenever it appears that "someone else pays," there is sure to be over-utilization of the service provided. The situation is exacerbated by the fact that medical technology has become more and more sophisticated and therefore much more expensive. With either government or private insurers paying the bill, there is little hesitation about applying the most sophisticated technology available even though there may be other, much less expensive and equally effective treatments available.[1]

The situation could be improved greatly if the patient or doctor faced a situation in which patients pay some share of the cost of extra treatment. They would then be less likely to engage in forms of treatment that are of marginal usefulness. This could be accomplished with higher deductibles and some limited cost-sharing by the patient —just what Ford recommended for Medicare.

If higher deductibles and cost-sharing would result in greater efficiency and lower prices for health care, one must ask why private insurers do not typically offer such policies. Generally, they offer instead small deductibles, if any at all, and no cost-sharing. In other words, the typical private insurance policy usually covers fairly modest, regular expenditures that could easily be anticipated and covered by the typical family. In this way, medical insurance departs significantly from the usual insurance concept where insurance is purchased to protect against unusual, catastrophic events.

---

[1] Martin Feldstein has said "there are two—and really only two—key ingredients to understanding the rise in hospital costs: the changing nature of the hospital product, and the impact of insurance. Of these, the second is the more crucial—and largely explains the first" (In "The High Cost of Hospitals—and What to Do About It," *Public Interest* [Summer 1977], p. 41).

The peculiar structure of medical insurance is primarily the result of our tax laws. Employers are allowed to provide medical insurance as a fringe benefit: the value of the policy does not represent taxable income to employees, but employers can deduct the costs from their tax bill. In this way, our tax system subsidizes the purchase of medical insurance.[2] However, it is obvious that the tax benefit is not very useful to workers unless they attach a high dollar value to health insurance. A policy that has high deductibles and significant cost-sharing would not have a high dollar value to the workers; a policy with low deductibles and no cost-sharing does.

Other forces also push us toward insurance policies with low patient cost-sharing. Prior to the advent of private health insurance, doctors had a difficult time collecting bills from their patients. With a high degree of cost-sharing this problem would presumably recur. Since doctors typically play a large role in the design and management of health insurance systems, there is a natural bias toward systems that avoid the bill collection problem.

However, the tax treatment of employer-provided health insurance probably remains dominant in explaining the structure of our current health insurance system. A great step forward might occur if only policies with high deductibles and greater cost-sharing were eligible for fringe benefit treatment. However, such a tax reform does not now appear to be politically feasible. There will thus be a tendency to seize on arbitrary reimbursement and price control mechanisms like those proposed by Ford and Carter. They will have some impact in slowing the rise in budget costs, and they may retard the development and application of more sophisticated medical technology. However, they will do this in a most inefficient manner and will perhaps lower the quality of care and reduce benefits from medical innovation.

There are other approaches to cost control that antedate Ford and Carter. One of the more promising is the health maintenance organization (HMO). This consists of a group of physicians who provide health care for a fixed annual fee. Such prepayment creates strong incentives for physicians to prescribe only those forms of treatment that have definite medical value. The federal government

---

[2] The resulting tax loss is estimated at almost $6 billion (see *Special Analyses, Budget of the United States, Fiscal Year 1978*, p. 128). The importance of the tax subsidy clearly emerges in E. B. Keeler, D. T. Morrow, and J. P. Newhouse, "The Demand for Supplementary Health Insurance, Do Deductibles Matter?" *Journal of Political Economy*, vol. 85 (August 1977), pp. 789–802. They show that if a national health insurance plan had moderate deductibles, people would be likely to buy insurance to cover the deductible if the insurance received a tax subsidy. Without subsidy, such purchases would be unlikely.

attempted to encourage HMOs with the Health Maintenance Organization Act of 1973 which provided for a five-year program to demonstrate the feasibility of the prepayment concept. By the end of 1978, 230 HMOs are expected to be operating, about half of which receive federal support. On the other hand, government has also imposed constraints on HMO development. The certification requirements for the grant program were extremely stringent and tended to increase capital investment requirements. As a result, HMOs were more expensive and less effective competitors than they might have been. HMOs may also have been constrained by 1974 legislation that created a network of health system agencies which, as one of their roles, attempt to reduce capital investment that duplicates existing health resources. While such planning may have some merit given the economic incentives facing our traditional health care delivery system, it may have a counterproductive impact if, as a byproduct, it restricts the expansion of the HMO delivery system.

There is considerable evidence that HMOs have been successful in lowering costs. A recent study suggests that they can lower members' expenses from 6 to 46 percent per year, primarily by reducing hospital utilization—up to 70 percent per person per year.[3] The key question is, of course, whether the quality of care suffers when an HMO is responsible for delivery. Evidence is difficult to collect on this issue, but to the extent that quality can be assessed there are considerable checks on the HMOs from institutions such as state licensing agencies, Professional Standards Review Organizations, and HEW for federally supported HMOs. The ultimate check on quality is, of course, consumer acceptance, and this will eventually determine whether the concept will prosper.

Other cost control institutions have already been mentioned in passing. Professional Standards Review Organizations consist of groups of physicians who evaluate their peers to assure quality care while limiting unnecessary treatment. Evaluations of such programs offer inconclusive results at this juncture, but some critics suggest that having physicians evaluate their peers may not be very effective without other incentives to improve efficiency.[4] The National Health Planning and Resources Development Act of 1974 established health system agencies which attempt to restrict capital expenditures on

---

[3] ICF, *Selected Use of Competition by Health System Agencies*, report submitted to HEW, contract HEW-HRA-23-75-0071 (Washington, D.C., 1977), pp. 11–13.

[4] For a critical analysis, see C. C. Havighurst and J. F. Blumstein, "Coping with Quality/Cost Trade-Offs in Medicare Care: The Role of PSROs," *Northwestern University Law Review*, vol. 70 (March-April 1975), pp. 6–68.

duplicative medical facilities in a region. Again, this is an attempt to provide a bureaucratic decision mechanism to replace market discipline where such discipline is eroded by the nature of the current insurance system. It is still too early to evaluate the effectiveness of the 1974 legislation, but conceptually, it does not offer much hope of controlling expenditures.[5]

National Health Insurance

> America needs to improve the way it pays for medical care. We should begin plans for a comprehensive national health insurance system. However, in view of the economic developments and the measures I have proposed to combat recession and inflation, I cannot now propose costly new programs. Once our current economic problems are behind us, the development of an adequate national medical insurance system should have high national priority.

This statement was made by Ford in his *Budget Message of the President* for fiscal 1976, presented in January 1975. For the next two years, he continued to struggle against the same economic and budget problems that prevented him from earlier proposing a comprehensive national health insurance program. No mention of national health insurance appeared in the next two Ford budgets.

The same statement could have been made in Carter's 1978 budget revisions. He, too, would like to offer a comprehensive national health insurance program, but he also wishes to control the size of the federal budget. Consequently, he wishes to slow down the rate of health cost increases prior to proposing a health insurance system. He does promise to make a proposal in early 1978, and while it seems virtually certain that he will, it will be interesting to see how long he will have to delay its full implementation.

One must ask why we have had so many health insurance proposals from both parties without ever getting one enacted. It may be that the making of proposals has become sort of a ritual while the need for comprehensive health insurance has slowly been withering away. The United States has now reached a standard of living and a level of medical technology in which it is difficult to argue that there is any strong relationship remaining between the availability of

---

[5] D. S. Salkever and T. W. Bigg, "Impact of State Certificate of Need Laws on Health Care Costs and Utilization" (Paper presented at Eastern Economic Association meeting, April 17, 1976).

medical care and the state of the nation's health. It is generally agreed that changes in lifestyle involving diet and exercise would have a far greater impact on life expectancy than the advent of national health insurance. Moreover, the implementation of Medicaid for the poor and Medicare for the elderly has taken care of the two groups who were most vulnerable to inadequate care in the past, while the spread of private insurance and the tax subsidy resulting from the deductibility of medical expenses in excess of 3 percent of adjusted gross income has provided considerable protection for the remaining population.

However, some gaps in coverage remain. The Congressional Budget Office estimates that there are 25 million people who have neither public nor private coverage. Eight million of these may be eligible for veterans' assistance, leaving 17 million whose only assistance is from the tax deductibility of medical expenses, which is useless for those without taxable income. The uncovered group tends to be concentrated among the self-employed, the unemployed, the chronically ill, students, and employees of small, low-wage businesses.[6] It is difficult to argue that this relatively small gap in coverage warrants the blunderbuss solution of national health insurance. Increased spending on 100 percent of the population solely to cure a problem that afflicts less than 10 percent does not make sense. We must look elsewhere to explain the continuing support for national health insurance.

It is my conjecture that the most important health problem perceived by ordinary citizens is exactly the same as that perceived by Ford and Carter. It is not that the public is generally receiving inadequate care; it is instead that the cost of care is soaring. The high costs leave the public vulnerable to financial catastrophe in the event of serious, long-term illnesses, because virtually all insurance policies impose some upper limit on the insurer's maximum liability.[7]

A large variety of bills and proposals has already been offered to deal with the problem of medical catastrophes. The costs depend very much on how catastrophe is defined and on how much recipients should be expected to pay out toward large and small medical bills. These options have been discussed extensively and will not be evalu-

---

[6] Congressional Budget Office, *Budget Options for Fiscal Year 1978*, February 1977, p. 151.

[7] Many other arguments have been advanced for the political appeal of national health insurance. An analysis can be found in Victor Fuchs, "From Bismark to Woodcock: The 'Irrational' Pursuit of National Health Insurance," *Journal of Law and Economics*, vol. 19 (August 1976), pp. 347–60.

ated here.[8] However, it is hard to imagine any approach that would succeed in redeeming Carter's promises and yet cost the federal budget less than about $7 billion.

This, for example, would be the cost of the Catastrophic Health Program and Medical Assistance Reform Bill (S. 2470), which would federalize medicaid. Uniform standards would be established across states and everyone would be covered whose medical expenditures lowered their remaining net income below Medicaid eligibility levels. If the eligibility standards matched those in the most generous existing state plans, the total costs would be $17 billion in fiscal 1978, but the extra federal costs would be lowered to $7.2 billion if states were required to maintain their current financial contributions to the program.

Most plans are very much more generous than this and their costs rise accordingly. The basic dilemma is that any plan that provides additional coverage will raise the demand for health care and will therefore impose greater upward pressure on the soaring costs that played an important role in creating the demand for national health insurance in the first place.

Putting the problem in its starkest terms, coverage cannot be extended to those currently uninsured and to catastrophic expenditures in general without absorbing a significant increase in the federal budget unless some way is found to reduce the consumption of medical care among those covered by already-existing private and public programs. The trick is to reduce the consumption of services that have "marginal value" while not affecting services that are "essential." This requires some sort of rationing, to which there are two very different approaches: increased government regulation or increased use of market incentives. We have already started down the regulatory path with the National Health Planning and Resources Development Act of 1974 and with the Carter price control proposals, which would eventually require some sort of complementary rationing mechanism to be really effective in controlling prices. Given our past efforts at regulating other industries, it is hard to be optimistic that such a mechanism can do a decent job at differentiating marginal from essential expenditures.

Greater reliance on the price mechanism has greater intellectual appeal, but as a first step, it would require eliminating the tax incen-

---

[8] See Congressional Budget Office, *Budget Options*, pp. 151–55; and Gordon Trapsnell, *A Comparison of the Costs of Major National Health Insurance Proposals*, prepared for the Department of Health, Education and Welfare, September 1976, PB-259-153.

tives to the first-dollar coverage now provided by our private insurance system. This would not be a panacea, however, because even in a totally efficient market, the relative price of medical care is likely to rise and it is very likely that total public and private spending would rise relative to GNP. In part, this is because health care is a typical labor-intensive service industry and with economic growth, the cost of labor will rise faster than the general price level. As the economy becomes wealthier, there would also be an increase in demand for care even if that demand were not subsidized. While the quality of care may also improve, our statistics will not measure such improvements properly, and the higher expenditures will show up as pure inflation in our data. Nevertheless, a change in the tax treatment of private insurance would have the salutory effect of slowing price increases and perhaps even reversing them temporarily.

While a change in tax policy does not seem politically feasible at the moment, the long-run alternatives are not exactly a politician's dream. The only possibilities are a cumbersome and inevitably inequitable regulatory apparatus or higher future taxes to finance continually soaring health costs. However we escape from this dilemma, Carter deserves considerable praise for moving slowly on the whole issue. There is much talk of a health crisis, but it is mostly hyperbole. In most areas of disease control, the nation's health has been on a long upward trend, and in those few areas where the trend has not been clearly upward, there is little to suggest that a lack of adequate care is the culprit. Severe difficulties remain in our health care delivery system, but the severest danger now is that we shall plunge into cures that are worse than the problems.

10
GRANTS-IN-AID

Particular components of the grants-in-aid system have already been touched upon. Chapter 6 notes that a large portion of President Carter's economic stimulus package takes the form of increased grants to state and local governments, and chapter 9 discusses President Ford's proposed reform of categorical health grants. One might ask why this study requires a separate chapter on a diverse set of programs that have very little in common other than that they are administered by states and localities but paid for by the federal government. A separate analysis is useful because the grants-in-aid system reflects a number of philosophical and economic themes that have been at the heart of disputes regarding the appropriate size and organization of the public sector in our society. There has been a continued and interesting war between two sets of forces that move in opposite directions. On one side are the pressures that lead to a proliferation of grant programs which enhances the power of the federal government; on the other are the pressures for consolidating grant programs in a way that enhances state and local discretion and simplifies programs. It is not clear who is winning this war. There are almost 500 categorical grant programs.[1] A large portion of these were created within the last ten years, but the Nixon and Ford administrations won a considerable number of battles in their efforts to implement the New Federalism philosophy by consolidating programs and initiating new general purpose and specific block grants. The implementation of General Revenue Sharing, Comprehensive Employment and Training block grants, Law Enforcement Assistance block grants, and Community Development block grants, all represent significant victories for the New Federalists.

---

[1] David B. Walker, "Categorical Grants: Some Clarifications and Continuing Concerns," *Intergovernmental Perspective*, vol. 3 (Spring 1977), p. 14.

Past Budget Trends

Grants-in-aid grew rapidly between the early 1950s and the early 1970s, both as a share of the federal budget and relative to state and local expenditures (see table 22). Between 1973 and 1976 there was a leveling off of both measures. The composition of grants has also changed significantly since the early 1950s. At that time grants related to payments to individuals constituted over 60 percent of the total and primarily consisted of public assistance programs such as AFDC and Old Age Assistance. In the late 1950s the interstate highway program increased the relative importance of the "other" category, and by 1960, payments to individuals fell to less than 40 percent of the total. After 1965 new transfer programs, such as Medicaid, caused the payments to individuals category to level off at almost 40 percent of the total, but after 1972 the relative importance of individual payments programs fell again to about a third of the total as General Revenue Sharing and other block grant programs added to the "other" category.

The change in composition also reflects the emergence of new priorities. For example, increased concern with the environment

Table 22

FEDERAL GRANTS-IN-AID OUTLAYS, FISCAL 1950–1976
(in billions of dollars)

| Year | Total Grants | Composition of Grants | | Grants as % of: | |
		Payments to Individuals	Other	Federal Outlays	State and Local Expenditures[a]
1950	$ 2.3	$ 1.4	$ 0.8	5.3	10.4
1955	3.2	1.8	1.4	4.7	10.1
1960	7.0	2.7	4.3	7.6	14.7
1965	10.9	4.0	7.0	9.2	15.3
1970	24.0	8.9	15.2	12.2	19.4
1971	28.1	10.8	17.3	13.3	19.9
1972	34.4	13.4	21.0	14.8	22.0
1973	41.8	13.1	28.7	17.0	24.3
1974	43.3	14.0	29.3	16.1	22.7
1975	49.7	16.1	33.6	15.3	23.2
1976	59.0	19.5	39.5	16.1	24.7

[a] As defined in the national income accounts.
Source: *Special Analyses, Budget of the United States Government, Fiscal Year 1978*, p. 273.

resulted in $2.4 billion in grants for sewage treatment plants in 1976, which will grow rapidly to $4.4 billion in 1977 and $5.2 billion in 1978. The composition also shifted because of the federalization in 1974 of the public assistance programs for the blind, disabled, and aged. Since that time, this set of needs has been served directly from the federal government through the Supplementary Security Income program and grants have been discontinued.

Since the late 1950s our grant system has tended to treat various states and regions more nearly equally whether measured on a grants per capita basis or on grants as a percentage of state personal income.[2] In part, this is due to the decline in the relative importance of highway grants and grants related to public lands. Both of these highly favor sparsely populated western states, while the newer general assistance and block grants tend to distribute the federal largesse more evenly.

Grants are allocated in a variety of ways. Formula distributions allocate General Revenue Sharing, Community Development, and other block grants, while with cost-sharing grants (covering up to 100 percent) depend on the extent to which a state or its localities decide to engage in particular federally supported activities. Many grants are hybrids which combine these two basic allocation mechanisms.

Cost-sharing grants do have some abstract appeal. Conceptually, the federal cost share should be directly related to the extent to which the benefits of a program in one state spill over and accrue to citizens of other states. However, there is no evidence that such a concept has played any role in determining cost shares in our current grant system. In most categorical programs the federal share is far higher than could be justified by spillover arguments. Of 437 programs studied by the Advisory Commission on Intergovernmental Relations, 158 required no state or local cost-sharing and fewer than 60 required states and localities to contribute 50 percent or more of costs.[3]

Despite the bewildering array of complex formulae that are used to distribute grants, the result is remarkably simple. The total amount of grants received by a particular state can be roughly predicted using only two variables—state population with the poverty population

[2] Over all states, excluding Alaska and Hawaii, the coefficient of variation of grants per capita has fallen from 0.50 in 1957 to 0.38 in 1967 to 0.20 in 1975. The coefficient of variation with respect to grants as a percentage of personal income has fallen from 0.53 in 1957 to 0.43 in 1967 to 0.26 in 1975.

[3] Cited in Office of Management and Budget, *Issues '78, Perspectives on Fiscal Year 1978 Budget*, 1977, p. 285.

weighted twice and state tax effort measured by state and local taxes as a percentage of personal income.[4] It does not logically follow that we could approximate today's distribution of grants by using a simple two-variable formula in place of the current army of bureaucrats and legions of grantsmen who interact to produce it. If one simple formula were used to distribute all grants, a new set of incentives would be created for lower levels of government. The distribution of grants would thus be altered and, perhaps more important, states and localities would significantly alter the composition of the basket of goods provided.

Categorical Grants and the Great Society

The Great Society's war on the social ills of the nation was implemented in large part through the categorical grants system. The so-called "welfare mess" is intimately related to the proliferation of programs that resulted. While the extent of the welfare mess may be very much exaggerated in recent discussions,[5] there is no doubt that much of the complexity and confusion in our current grant system is the result of a tendency to plunge into specific social programs with the best of intentions but without much thought as to how each program relates to other programs or to the nation's overall social goals.

A fundamental choice was made when it was decided that the war on poverty should be fought using in-kind programs which are inherently cumbersome. A complex set of regulations is required, first, to ensure that the program really increases the consumption of things like food and medical care, and second, to reduce the probability of corruption among the providers. The providers, of course, have an intense interest in the design of the programs, and their lobbying efforts sometimes distort the effectiveness of the programs

---

[4] For 1975, the regression equation is
$$G = 1092.3 + 0.20P = 65.8T$$
$$(38.9) \quad (5.5)$$
Where
G = total grants,
P = population plus the poverty population, and
T = tax effort as defined above.
The figures in brackets represent T scores. (This formula was suggested by Roger Kaufman.)

[5] Frederick Doolittle, Frank Levy, and Michael Wiseman reach this conclusion in "The Mirage of Welfare Reform," *Public Interest* (Spring 1977), pp. 62–87.

from the point of view of the recipients. For example, home builders push new home construction for serving low- and moderate-income groups when it is probably possible to develop more equitable and efficient housing programs that utilize the existing housing stock more extensively. We face still another problem in the American three-branch system of government. Different congressional committees have jurisdiction over different in-kind programs. As a result, individual programs tend to be developed without sufficient attention to their impact on other existing programs.

However, all this does not fully explain the incredible complexity of our current system. In large part it stems from carrying the in-kind philosophy to its logical extremes. Once the goal of trying to increase a particular group's consumption of a particular good or service is accepted, there is no limit to arguments for focusing programs more and more narrowly. Our food programs provide an excellent illustration of this. The basic program for satisfying food needs is the food stamp program. It is supposed to ensure that no family has to spend more than 30 percent of its net income on obtaining an adequate diet. While the administration of the program is often attacked and while it does have some dubious structural features, it is, in its basic philosophy, a fairly good program. It is the main welfare program for the working poor of the nation and it probably accomplishes its redistributive goals without a major negative impact on work effort.

However, Congress was not satisfied that the program serves all food needs. It therefore created a multitude of other supplementary food programs for specially defined groups. Hence, we have special programs for the elderly, such as Meals on Wheels; we have a special program for pregnant or lactating mothers, infants, and children up to five years old (WIC); and we have fifteen additional programs that subsidize school lunches and various other kinds of meals for children. These very narrow, special programs have a number of common characteristics. With the exception of the basic school lunch program, they tend to be very small relative to the food stamp program. Whether or not the eligible population is served depends largely on whether states or localities have chosen to participate in the program. For example, the plethora of school lunch programs fails to reach about 700,000 children from below-poverty-line families, because some states or localities have decided that it is not worthwhile to participate. Because some of the programs are small and complicated, administrative costs tend to be high relative to the value of the benefit provided. For example, administrative expenses absorb more than 20 percent of the WIC program's total cost. Programs such as those for the elderly and school lunch programs are not generally related to need. Consequently, they serve rich and poor alike.

While I have used food programs for illustration, exactly the same story could be told with regard to our health, education, and housing programs. In each area, there is a multitude of programs focused on a narrowly defined need. Often they are small and serve only a tiny proportion of the eligible population. There are, in fact, so many programs that it is no exaggeration to say that we have lost track of the interactions among them. Any attempt to determine what we have done to the national distribution of income in the decade since the initiation of the Great Society faces extraordinary conceptual and statistical difficulties. Undoubtedly, the multitude of programs has greatly benefited the poor. But it is equally certain that there are more efficient and equitable ways of accomplishing the same goals.

As this is written, Carter is about to propose a welfare reform program that may introduce some order into this complex array of programs, but it is not yet possible to comment on the details of his program. However, it should be noted that the grants-in-aid system extends far beyond the social programs. There is a complex system of economic development grants—some focused on rural areas, some on cities, and some directed to depressed areas. There are grants for fish and wildlife conservation, for coastal zone development, for highways, for subways, for the arts and humanities, and on and on. Each tries to enhance a specific type of economic activity, but in a full employment economy this can only be done at the expense of some other activity. Because the whole system is so complex, it is impossible to determine the system's overall impact on the allocation of resources. In any case budget decisions are for the most part made one program at a time, and only marginal adjustments to the system are possible.

Occasionally, there are more radical proposals. Carter's forthcoming welfare reform package may move social programs slightly away from the in-kind concept and toward a greater use of cash payments. His recent food stamp proposals would make the system more like a cash grant, giving recipients more flexibility in the use of their income. However, it seems likely that the in-kind concept will continue to dominate the provisions of health services, education grants, and housing subsidies. Consequently, we shall continue to have a complex system of social grants-in-aid complemented by hundreds of grant programs for economic development and other purposes.

130

Ford's Block Grant Proposals

Ford made a small step toward simplifying the grant system in his budgets of 1977 and 1978. His proposals were not radical, but they received little attention from the public, the press, or the Congress. As manifested in the 1978 budget, the proposals involved consolidating a very small portion of the total array of grant programs into three block grants:

- 23 education programs were to be consolidated into a single block grant in the Financial Assistance for Elementary and Secondary Education Act.
- 15 child nutrition programs were to be consolidated into a single grant focused on needy children.
- 20 health programs, including Medicaid, were to be consolidated into one block grant by the Financial Assistance for Health Care Act.

While the Ford program would have achieved considerable simplification and provoked states and localities to define their own needs, it was also motivated, in large part, by a wish to restrain the federal budget. The severe constraints that would have been imposed on federal support for Medicaid have already been described. The child nutrition program would have saved more than $1 billion by focusing assistance on the low-income population. The Ford program would have provided aid to the 700,000 children from low-income families who now get no school lunch subsidies, but subsidies would be taken away from the middle class and rich.

Ford might have proposed an even more radical reform. Given that the size of the food stamp subsidy depends on family size and is supposed to provide for an adequate diet, one might argue that food stamps should be used to purchase school lunches. With such an arrangement, the federal government could get out of the school lunch business. However, Ford avoided this draconian solution and continued child nutrition assistance as a complement to the food stamp program.

The Ford proposals represent a further extension of the New Federalism initiated by the Nixon administration. Nixon's General Revenue Sharing, while almost totally unrestricted, was, in part, a substitute for a further expansion of the categorical grant system. The New Federalism concept tends to be attacked from both ends of the political spectrum although the most vigorous attacks tend to come from liberals who worry that, if states and localities are given more freedom to allocate grant resources, they will direct funds away from social programs for the needy. Conservatives tend to be more sympathetic to the New Federalism approach, but there are many who feel that if the states and localities have the freedom to spend the money they should also have the responsibility to raise it by increasing their own taxes. Conservatives also worry that unrestricted block grants will have the effect of expanding the public sector, because with federal subsidies the residents of states and localities will think that they are getting more for their state and local tax bill than they really are when federal taxes are considered. More directly, the General Revenue Sharing formula and the distribution formulae for many block grants bases the distribution of funds partly on state tax effort, which might encourage a higher level of taxes than would otherwise prevail.

The evidence on General Revenue Sharing does suggest that the liberal fears have some foundation. Richard Nathan and his associates note that "recipient governments have, in fact, put relatively little emphasis on social service programs" such as legal aid, job training, and housing assistance. They do, however, note that the poor have benefited significantly from some of the more general applications of revenue sharing funds to health, recreation, and education.[6]

The conservative case is harder to assess. Many jurisdictions have used a large portion of their General Revenue Sharing funds to reduce taxes, to avoid tax increases, or to avoid borrowing.[7] However, some of the funds are used for new spending. Therefore, the total state and local government sector is larger with revenue sharing than without it. But this may not be the real policy choice. As already noted, revenue sharing and block grants may be a substitute for increases in cost-sharing categorical grants, which probably have an even greater expansionary impact on state and local spending.[8]

The Ford block grants do meet the liberal argument, in part, in that they are strongly oriented toward need. Variables such as the low-income population and per capita income play a large role in their distribution formulae, and the restraints on spending in the child nutrition program are to the relative benefit of the poor. But it

---

[6] Richard P. Nathan et al., *Revenue Sharing: The Second Round* (Washington, D.C.: Brookings Institution, 1977), pp. 70–71.

[7] Richard P. Nathan et al., *Monitoring Revenue Sharing* (Washington, D.C.: Brookings Institution, 1975), p. 232.

[8] Advisory Commission on Intergovernmental Relations, *Federal Grants: Their Effect on State-Local Expenditures, Employment Levels, Wage Rates* (Washington, D.C., 1977), p. 46.

must be admitted that the health block grant would restrict Medicaid spending on the poor. The liberals' opposition to the Ford program clearly indicates their opinion that, on balance, the poor will do better with a continuation of the current categorical programs.

It is not yet clear where the Carter administration is going on the grants-in-aid issue. The February budget revisions did not accept the Ford reforms, but indicated that they would be studied. Because the Carter economic stimulus program is implemented largely through grants, they soar from $59.0 billion in 1976 to $72.4 billion in 1977 and to $81.7 billion in Carter's 1978 budget. As the stimulus program phases out, the Carter long-run budget envisions a decline in the relative importance of grants, but $5.5 billion from the stimulus program is reserved in a contingency account to finance the previously discussed welfare reform package. These funds could easily find their way back into the grant system.

PART THREE
THE INSTITUTIONAL RESPONSE

11
REFORM OF THE BUDGET PROCESS

Concern over the growth in government spending may not yet have resulted in any massive budget cutting, but it has provoked a number of legislative and institutional responses that seek to restrain spending and to bring more rationality to bear on policy making. These responses include the enactment of the Congressional Budget and Impoundment Control Act of 1974, the introduction of numerous "Sunset Laws" which seek to terminate programs that have outlived their usefulness, and the development of zero-base budgeting mechanisms within the Carter administration.

The New Congressional Budget Process

President Nixon, frustrated by his inability to control the growth of the federal budget, refused to spend all of the money appropriated by Congress. Although presidents had impounded funds throughout our history, Nixon's more vigorous use of the impoundment mechanism was soon challenged by Congress and in the courts.

However, the congressional argument against impoundment was weakened by the fact that congressional decision procedures did not contain any explicit mechanism for controlling budget totals. Each bill affecting spending was considered separately, while receipts totals were the result of votes on individual pieces of tax and other revenue legislation. It should not be concluded that the totals had no influence on the deliberations. The presidents' January budget recommendations to Congress had considerable influence on the outcome, and of course, presidential budgets have long contained an explicit aggregate fiscal policy. Congress also had a mechanism for recommending an overall fiscal strategy in the Joint Economic Committee, but this committee has no explicit legislative powers. Consequently, except for those rare occasions where overall spending limits were imposed, Congress never explicitly voted on overall spending and receipts totals.[1] There was not, therefore, a rigorous link between the totals and the size of individual programs.

The new Congressional Budget and Impoundment Control Act of 1974 redressed this deficiency by establishing a procedure to force votes imposing a ceiling on budget authority and outlays and setting a floor under receipts. The legislation established a Senate and a House Budget Committee. At the same time, a Congressional Budget Office (CBO) was created to provide technical advice and research resources.

By March 15 of every year the various standing committees of the Congress are to submit reports on budget estimates to the budget committees. This process is analogous to the departmental budget requests submitted to the Office of Management and Budget during the late summer in the executive branch budget process. By April 1 the CBO must submit a fiscal policy report to the budget committees. On the basis of the fiscal policy report and the budget estimates from the standing committees, the budget committees prepare the First Budget Resolution which establishes targets for total budget authority, outlays and receipts, and also establishes targets for each budget function. Congress must pass the First Budget Resolution by May 15.

The budget targets are to guide the various congressional committees as they work on appropriations and tax legislation. Action is supposed to be completed on all money bills by early September. By September 15, Congress must pass a Second Budget Resolution. While the First Resolution only establishes targets, the Second Resolution establishes a binding ceiling on budget authority and outlays and a floor for receipts. If the ceilings and floor are inconsistent with the receipts and appropriations actions taken prior to September 15, the resolution may contain directives to the relevant committees to alter their totals. Reconciling legislation is to be passed by September 25, a few days before the new fiscal year begins on October 1.

After the Second Budget Resolution is passed, any legislation that attempts to raise spending in the subsequent fiscal year can be

---

[1] There is a statutory limit on the public debt and the debate on this limit is often an occasion to vent antispending sentiments. It is probably safe to conclude, however, that the debt limit does not exercise any real constraints since it has to accommodate spending and receipts actions which are, for all practical purposes, *faits accomplis.*

subject to a point of order. If any such legislation is passed, it is necessary to pass simultaneously an amended budget resolution. The resolution can also be amended independently if it is believed that changing conditions warrant a change in fiscal policy or if something else happens to warrant higher spending or lower receipts.

The new congressional budget process has now been in effect for three budgets. The first round, for fiscal 1976, was officially a "trial run," but for all practical purposes, Congress acted as though the procedure were binding.

Has the new procedure slowed the growth in spending? It is too early to say, and indeed, a definitive answer may never be possible. An answer requires knowing what would have happened in the absence of the new procedure, and that is always difficult. We do know that during the Ford administration, the First Budget Resolution consistently provided an outlay ceiling significantly above the level recommended by the President. For fiscal 1976, the President recommended $349.4 billion in outlays; the First Resolution specified $367.0 billion. For fiscal 1977, the comparable numbers were $394.2 billion and $413.3 billion.

But, while these 1976 and 1977 budgets were being formulated, the economy was suffering severely from the aftermath of the 1974–1975 recession. Without the new budget procedures it is conceivable that the response to high unemployment levels would have been less disciplined. In other words, Ford's 1976 and 1977 budgets might have been exceeded by even larger amounts had it not been for the new procedure.

After Carter took over, the congressional budget was quickly adapted to his policies. A Third 1977 Resolution was passed to accommodate his economic stimulus package, raising the Second Resolution's $413.1 billion to $417.5 billion. When the President withdrew his tax rebate proposal, there was much consternation that he was raising havoc with the new congressional procedure, but Congress eventually yielded and passed what was, in effect, a Fourth Resolution at $409.2 billion.

The vacillation of the President and Congress with regard to the 1977 budget can be charitably interpreted as revealing great flexibility in response to changing economic conditions, or it can be less generously interpreted as revealing potential weaknesses in the process. The latter interpretation would be stronger if all of the amendments had been in an upward direction, but, of course, they were not.

While the experience with the 1977 budget may not itself reveal weakness, it does at least illustrate a severe potential danger to the process. If the Second Resolution begins to be amended routinely in response to small variations in economic indicators or in presidential policy, the restraints imposed by the budget process will soon wither away.

Unfortunately, there will be strong pressures for frequent amendments in the future. One problem with the procedure is that amendments to the Second Resolution may be necessitated by estimating errors rather than by changes in policy. Estimating outlays and receipts is always difficult. Outlays for entitlement programs are very sensitive to economic conditions, but even if the economic forecast is correct, outlay estimates may be in error because more or fewer people than expected demand benefits in programs such as food stamps, Medicare, and social security. Or erroneous guesses may be made for political purposes. The new procedure does not differentiate amendments necessitated by estimating errors from those required by policy changes, and it is possible that amendments necessitated by estimating problems may provide an excuse for changes in policy.

Estimating difficulties are well illustrated by the new procedure's experience with the 1976 budget. The First Resolution passed in May 1975 specified an outlay ceiling of $367.0 billion. By September it was thought necessary to raise the ceiling to $374.9 billion, not because of new policy initiatives but because of changes in estimates. Because of a spending shortfall, the actual total for 1976 came out at $365.7 billion—actual outlays were in fact lower than those prescribed by the First Resolution. It also appears that the 1977 totals will come out lower than prescribed by the Amended Third Resolution.

It is, however, inevitable that we shall eventually face a situation in which estimating errors work the other way and the Second Resolution will be exceeded unless programs are cut back to remain within the Second Resolution's ceiling or the resolution is amended to accommodate estimating errors. If spending cutbacks ever occur to offset estimating errors, this will be a clear sign that the new budget procedure is exercising a strong restraining influence on total government spending. It is, however, more likely that the resolution will be amended.

There are more fundamental flaws in the new procedures. In order to avoid denuding the appropriations committees of too much power, the House and Senate Budget Committees have refrained from delving very much into program detail. (Although it should be noted that the House Committee has shown somewhat less restraint than the Senate Committee.) Hence, the budget committees have set authority and outlay ceilings on each budget function and have, for the most part, left the development of program details to the authorization and appropriations committees.

The problem is that it is very difficult to establish functional totals in a logical manner without a thorough examination of the programmatic issues underlying them. Budgeting involves the resolution of thousands of very detailed issues. One must ask questions like how many more forest rangers can be justified next year? If more can be justified, should we add to total spending for the natural resources function or can we reduce another program? If the functional total goes up, should we reduce some other function? If so, which program is of least value? In the executive branch's budget process only a fraction of the thousands of potential program issues are examined with care, but nevertheless there is enough detailed programmatic analysis to cause constant iteration between the consideration of program details and total spending. It is, in fact, hard to understand the implications of a spending addition or reduction in a budget function without knowing the implications for specific programs.

In the congressional budget process there is some room for iteration between program detail and functional totals during the interval between the First and Second Resolution. However, the details and the functional totals are considered by different people, with the details handled by the appropriations committees and the functional totals by the budget committees. It is hard to believe that this separation of duties will not lead to irrationalities in the consideration of the myriad of trade-offs that have to be resolved in any budget process that truly imposes spending restraints.

That is not to say that the executive branch process is free of irrationalities. The federal budget is so complex that it is humanly impossible to consider all potential trade-offs which theoretically number in the millions. Shortcuts are necessary in any rational process, and no one would claim that the many shortcuts taken in the executive branch process necessarily represent the best approach possible.

Another problem afflicts both the executive branch and Congressional processes. For all practical purposes, budgeting occurs one year at a time. The law requires five-year projections of the spending implications of any new programs and of total spending in the congressional and presidential budgets. Such projections play some role in the formation of the president's budget, and President Ford provided in the 1978 budget an unusually detailed analysis of its implications for the development of the 1979 budget. However, the analysis was far from complete and the executive branch is a long way from multiyear budgeting. As for Congress, there is little evidence that the five-year projections have had any significant influence on the budget process. While five-year projections have been printed in committee reports, they have not yet been published in the conference report which guides the final vote on budget resolutions. The lack of multiyear budgeting clearly biases the process in favor of programs that have minor spending implications at first, but then grow mightily in the long run.

Despite its deficiencies, the new congressional budget process may already have had some successes. Many believe that the Tax Reform Act of 1976 would have contained more special-interest provisions were it not for the receipts constraint imposed by the budget resolutions. The budget process also focused attention on the irrationality of the "1 percent" kicker that overcompensated civil service pensioners for increases in the cost of living, and the program was reformed. However, as noted earlier, it is impossible to prove beyond any doubt that these things would not have occurred in the absence of the new process. Any evidence that the process has been successful will remain impressionistic for a long time to come.

Zero-Base Budgeting and Sunset Laws

One of the most important constraints on bringing rationality to the budget results from the bureaucracy's reluctance to specify goals for programs and to evaluate their success in achieving these goals. Because the output of government programs is typically very difficult to measure, decision makers tend to be helpless unless they get the cooperation of bureaucrats, who have a virtual monopoly over the information relevant to the evaluation of programs. All presidents have tussled with this problem and over the past fifteen years there have been a number of formal attempts to cope with it. President Johnson invented planning-programming-budgeting-systems (PBBS); President Nixon had management by objectives (MBO); and President Ford tried presidential management initiatives (PMI) just before he left office. President Carter has recently launched zero-base budgeting (ZBB) and Congress has gotten into the act with the Sunset Laws (SL). While these various approaches differ significantly in their details, they contain one common goal: they all attempt to force periodic evaluations of government programs on a bureaucracy that would rather not be bothered and that often—and sometimes correctly—blames the Congress for not providing clear program goals.

ZBB forces departments to divide up their programs into decision units. Objectives must be defined for the units and the implications of adding or reducing spending on the unit must be evaluated. For each program, a minimum budget level at which the program can be effective is specified. Options specifying various increases in programs above the minimum level are ranked along with options that would eliminate programs entirely. A budget restraint is then established and one proceeds down the list of ranked options until an acceptable budget total is reached.

A number of SL bills are now being considered by Congress. The most prominent was introduced by Senator Muskie (S.2) with an identical bill being introduced by Congressman Blanchard (HR 1756) in the House. All the SL bills force a periodic evaluation of all government spending programs. Some also force a review of tax expenditures.

ZBB and SL face the same formidable problems that caused the demise of PPBS and MBO and which may have done in PMI if Ford had remained in office. Even if evaluations can be forced upon a reluctant bureaucracy, a large portion of the evaluations will not be very useful. Most government programs are inherently difficult to evaluate. With only a few exceptions when user charges are levied, the output of government programs never face the test of the market-place. There is no price at which the output is traded, so there is no direct way to value it. Proxies for market prices must be developed and there are often a variety of ways in which they can be formulated. By choosing assumptions appropriately, the clever bureaucrat can often turn the evaluation into an advocacy document for the program. Busy policymaking officials often do not have the time to differentiate good from bad evaluations, given that ZBB and SL, like PBBS, will generate a veritable flood of paperwork. It was, in fact, a flood of shoddy paperwork that eventually drowned PPBS.

It was hoped that ZBB would avoid the elaborate evaluations produced by PPBS, but the ranking procedure described above is so complex that it is difficult to handle in short papers. Preliminary indications are that even minor agencies are producing massive documents.

Even if good evaluations are eventually produced, they will not necessarily cause the termination of bad programs. Bad programs generally exist for good political reasons, often because they benefit particular powerful constituencies. One could not find a better example than part B of the education impact aid program, which provides financial assistance to counties that have federal civil servants living in them. There is no strong evidence that these residents impose a particular burden on a community and much of the aid goes to some of the richest counties in the nation—those surrounding Washington, D.C. Every President from Truman to Carter has zero-base budgeted this program and decided that the sun should set on it. While this is written, the program is still contained in an education appropriations bill now being considered by Congress.

Programs like impact aid create severe doubts that ZBB and SL will succeed where their predecessors failed. An important weakness of such mechanisms is that they take a blunderbuss approach to the problem. They attempt to evaluate all government programs according to a rigid schedule. This results in a lot of wasted motion. Not much will be gained from overall evaluations of highly popular, generally efficient programs, such as social security, even though some narrow aspects of the program may be in need of evaluation. Similarly, there seems to be little hope in the first instance of getting rid of certain highly popular inefficient programs such as impact aid.

ZBB and SL would have more chance of success if they were based on a carefully thought out set of priorities for doing evaluations. We are genuinely uncertain about the effectiveness of many programs. These are prime candidates for evaluation and the evaluation may have some impact on whether or not they are continued. I am suggesting, in other words, that the effort be more focused. This provides less chance that the bureaucracy can drown the system in a sea of useless paper. Ford took this approach in the PMI system by forcing cabinet secretaries to identify a specific, but limited, number of programs for evaluation each year. Committee amendments to the Muskie SL bill move in this direction by establishing a mechanism for making some evaluations more intense than others, but some sort of evaluation still has to be provided for all programs.

Of course, a more limited approach would face many of the same obstacles as the broad approach of ZBB and SL. Departments would have a strong tendency to identify only their best programs as candidates for evaluations. Even where dubious programs were selected, there would be a strong tendency to produce evaluations that were nothing more than advocacy documents. However, with a more limited flow of paper, decision makers would have more chance to differentiate good evaluations from propaganda, and the President could focus his scorn on those cabinet secretaries whose departments were clearly doing a bad job.

Cover and book design: Pat Taylor